WHITE ONION SOUP ASPARAGUS
RAW FENNEL & COURGETTE PRUNE & ARMAGNAC
PEA SOUP A LA FRANCA... QUAIL
CHAKCHOUKA PRU... QUAIL
WITH MERGUEZ CHICKEN LEMON POLENTA TERRINE SNAIL
POTTED OXTAIL SMOKED CHICKE...
CRAB, CORN, GINGER GRAND MARNIE...
& CHILLI RISOTTO ROLLED LAMB
GOATS' CHEESE BEETROOT RAVIOL...
SLOW-BAKED ONIONS PEARS, ROQUEFOR...
PEA PANCAKES CREPES SUZETT...
SAUCE GRIBICHE GREEN LENTILS
LOBSTER SALAD « WATEGO » JAM...
SMOOTH CHICKEN RIZ...
LIVER PATE SALAD WITH HORSERADISH SAL...
DRESSING PICKLED CABBAG...
PARTRIDG...
GORGONZOLA, WALNUT & ...
BACON STUFFED MUSHROOMS POACHED PEAR...
PISSALADIERE WITH VIETNAMESE DRESSIN...
MARINATED SARDINE FILLETS PROVENCAL TIA...
KAFFIR LIME ICED PARFAIT SALTED CARAM...
SOUSED MACKEREL EGG PATES DU...

BRUNO LOUBET MANGE TOUT

BRUNO LOUBET MANGE TOUT

EBURY
PRESS

To my parents,
Mauricette and Clement,
who taught me from an early age
how to value and appreciate
what the land has to offer.

10 9 8 7 6 5 4 3 2 1

Published in 2013 by Ebury Press, an imprint of Ebury Publishing

A Random House Group Company

The Random House Group Limited Reg. No. 954009

Addresses for companies within the Random House Group can be found at www.
randomhouse.co.uk

A CIP catalogue record for this book is available from the British Library

The Random House Group Limited supports the Forest Stewardship Council®
(FSC®), the leading international forest-certification organisation. Our books
carrying the FSC label are printed on FSC®-certified paper. FSC is the only
forest-certification scheme supported by the leading environmental organisations,
including Greenpeace. Our paper procurement policy can be found at www.
randomhouse.co.uk/environment

To buy books by your favourite authors and register for offers visit
www.randomhouse.co.uk

Design by Will Webb
Photography by Jonathan Lovekin
Props styling by Sanjana

Printed and bound in China by Toppan Leefung

ISBN 9780091950477

CONTENTS

INTRODUCTION

I was born in south-west France, in the Gironde region, and spent my first 19 years in Libourne, a small country town. Situated at the junction of the Dordogne and the Isle rivers it started life as a small fishing village. It later grew in size and importance as the region began producing wine, taking advantage of the varied soils and landscapes. Nowadays a large part of the land is carpeted with long rows of vineyards, which follow the curves of the hills and plains, and elegant beige stone houses scattered around – the 'châteaux'. Wine is the lifeblood of the town and without it everything would stop.

My father's family was from the Pyrenees and my mother's from the Périgord, so my upbringing was mostly influenced by these three regions of the great South West. This is the land of foie gras, truffles, geese, ducks, game birds, wild mushrooms, crayfish, fine wines and much more. In fact, the Gironde Estuary is even home to sturgeons, which are also farmed in the area and give us the sumptuously elegant *caviar d'Aquitaine*. The unusual abundance and diversity of the South West's fine produce and the straightforward, no-nonsense character of its people has made this region renowned all over the world.

My father was an extremely hard worker: his official job was with the French railway, but he also worked, unofficially, farming land. Sixty to seventy hours' work a week was the price my dad was prepared to pay for his children to have what he called the 'supplements'. He was a man of few words. Buying a wheel of Pyrenees cheese or good fishing tackle, or taking us to Arcachon to open oysters under a pine tree with a bottle of Entre-Deux-Mers wine were his ways of participating in our education and showing us love. My parents were children during the Second World War so hardship and deprivation were anchored in their memories as ghosts who could always come back, and thus we learned to appreciate everything, especially food. We certainly didn't waste anything and lived life according to the seasons.

I remember my dad telling us he would have loved to have been a chef and travelled to places like New York, but in the end London was the furthest he ever went. In hindsight, I think his unfulfilled ambition was the spark that prompted me to make a change and have a different life, so at the tender age of 14 I enrolled as an apprentice chef at a Bordeaux catering school for three years. The starting point for French cooking was the country's wonderful diversity of regions, each making the most of its environment and bringing out the flavours

from its great local produce, the fruits of its 'terroir'. But early in my career I realised that the knowledge needed to be an accomplished chef was not just about your surroundings, your local culture and ingredients, but also about breaking out of your comfort zone – understanding and embracing other cultures to enrich your own. This vision has taken me on a long culinary journey, learning from and working for special people like Ramon Pajares, Raymond Blanc and Pierre Koffmann, and working in many different styles of kitchen across the world.

We probably all have childhood food memories that we cherish. What I find amazing is that the food of these memories always seems to taste better than that which we tuck into today. Is it fair to say that the ingredients used to be better and therefore the end result was tastier? That our mother and grandmother used to spend more time in their kitchen? Mine certainly did; I was very fortunate! Often, the smell of a stew or soup wafting around the house would welcome us back from school. I remember my grandmother saying: 'A good soup brings the men home!' And who could fail to be entranced by the complex aroma of a beef daube simmering on the stove; the sweet, spicy and buttery smell of baked apples; or the yeasty creamy scent of a baking brioche – long, slow cooking with layers of flavour?

I believe that some classic recipes cannot be improved and will remain true to their origins throughout the ages. But I also feel some dishes can have an extended life if they're given a little twist. I have been fortunate in my work to travel a lot, which has enabled me to feed my inspiration with elements from other cultures, integrating them into my cooking and giving me a new 'palate of flavours'. Perhaps the most influential period of my life was my time in Brisbane, Australia. I left England in 2001 for a new life Down Under and spent eight years adopting the Aussie way. When I arrived there, I was faced with a situation where I was not Bruno from London but the new French guy from London who had to prove himself. So I put my head down and worked hard to cook what people expected, but always, where possible, bringing an element of surprise. In a certain way I had to simplify my cooking and refocus, which was a great exercise and certainly helped me with the rebirth of Bistrot Bruno Loubet in London.

I came back to England and after six months of hunting for the perfect pub in Oxfordshire or Hampshire, I met Mark Sainsbury and Michael Benyan, the owners of the successful Zetter Hotel in Clerkenwell, London. The alchemy between us was natural and resulted in a business partnership. Mark and Michael opened the door of their business to me and Bistrot Bruno Loubet was born.

And now at the age of 50, I feel I have a strong sense of belonging in terms of my food. London is a fantastic metropolis – multicultural and in constant evolution, which makes it the ideal background for what I love to do. This book is a collection of my favourite recipes from 50 years of culinary and cultural heritage: some new, some old and many adapted to make cooking them at home quick and easy. All in their way reflect the layers of experience I have gathered from my work and life and I hope you will enjoy cooking them as much as I have done over the years.

WHITE ONION SOUP
PEA SOUP
SNAILS & MEATBALLS
MAURICETTE
WHOLE ARTICHOKE BAKE
RAW FENNEL &
COURGETTE SALAD
CHAKCHOUKA
WITH MERGUEZ
POTTED OXTAIL
CRAB, CORN, GINGER
& CHILLI RISOTTO
GRILLED & SMOKED
AUBERGINES
GOATS' CHEESE &
SOFT GREENS QUICHE
SPRING OEUFS EN GELEE
SLOW-BAKED ONIONS
GORGONZOLA, WALNUT &
BACON STUFFED MUSHROOMS

PEA PANCAKES & POACHED EGG
LOBSTER SALAD
SMOOTH CHICKEN
LIVER PATE
COUNTRY-STYLE PATE
CHICKEN TERRINE
PISSALADIERE WITH
MARINATED SARDINE FILLETS
SOUSED MACKEREL
SPICED SALMON TARTARE
ASPARAGUS ROASTED
WITH MEAT JUS
BEETROOT RAVIOLI 1997
GREEN LENTILS
SMOKED CHICKEN
LEMON & SPINACH DUMPLINGS
STILTON FRITTERS

STARTERS

WHITE ONION SOUP
WITH LOVAGE PESTO

A traditional Italian pesto is made from basil and lightly toasted pine kernels but I've given the dish an English character by substituting these for lovage and pumpkin seeds. The flavour of lovage is somewhere between celery and parsley but it's also a lot stronger, so a little goes a long way. Lovage is a wonderful herb but sadly, and somewhat surprisingly given how easy it is to grow, it can be difficult to find. If you can't get hold of it then replace the quantity below with a mixture of celery leaves (two thirds) and parsley (one third). Lovage does give the dish a delicious and unique twist, so I'd urge you to seek it out. Or grow your own!

Serves 6

60g butter
500g onions, finely sliced
2 garlic cloves
½ tsp fresh thyme leaves
1 tbsp plain flour
80ml dry white wine
800ml milk
½ bay leaf

Lovage pesto
2 tbsp flaked almonds
4 tbsp pumpkin seeds
2 garlic cloves
125ml olive oil
1 tbsp cider vinegar
2 handfuls of lovage
60g Grana Padano or Parmesan cheese
salt and black pepper

In a casserole, melt the butter until foaming, then add the onions, garlic and thyme and season with salt. Give everything a good stir then cover with a lid. Lower the heat to allow the onions to soften slowly without developing any colour. Stir from time to time but not too often.

After 20 minutes, remove the lid and stir well. Cook with the lid off for 3–4 minutes to let any remaining liquid evaporate, then stir in the flour. Cook for 2 minutes, stirring continuously, then add the white wine and bring to the boil. Do not worry if the mixture becomes quite thick, adding the milk will thin it. Add the milk along with the bay leaf and mix well with a whisk. Cover with a lid and leave to simmer for 20 minutes.

While the soup is simmering away happily, make the pesto. Lightly toast the almonds and pumpkin seeds in a dry frying pan until pale golden. Immediately remove from the pan and spread them out on a flat, cold surface to stop them cooking and cool. Once cool, place the almonds and pumpkin seeds in a food processor or blender, along with the garlic, olive oil and vinegar. Blend to a fine texture, then add the lovage and Grana Padano. Blend for another 30 seconds or until smooth and green. Season to taste.

Fish the bay leaf out of the soup and discard. Blend the soup until smooth then pass through a fine sieve for the ultimate velvety texture. Return to the pan to reheat gently. Serve with a spoonful of pesto drizzled over each portion.

BRUNO'S TIPS

I suggest you make a larger quantity of the pesto (four times the quantities given here) so that you can store it in a jar in the fridge, ready to use with pasta, a tomato salad or even roasted vegetables. It will keep for up to a week in the fridge if stored in a sterilised jar.

PEA SOUP A LA FRANCAISE

Let's be honest, how many of you like to buy peas in their pods and spend hours having to shell them before eating them? There is sometimes a pre-conceived negativity towards buying frozen vegetables, but in the case of peas and broad beans, this is simply ridiculous. Most frozen peas and broad beans are actually better than fresh. If you buy the very small frozen peas (petit pois), they can taste amazing. The technology behind the freezing process is so advanced that peas can be frozen in bags only a few hours after being picked, so it goes without saying that they will be superior to a box of peas that has travelled and been stored in different places over time before being sold. Unless you grow peas yourself or buy them directly from a grower, you are better off buying good-quality frozen ones.

Serves 6

80g butter
1 onion, chopped
2 garlic cloves, chopped
1 tbsp fresh thyme leaves
1.2 litres light chicken stock
400g frozen petit pois, defrosted
olive oil, to serve
salt and black pepper

Garnish

300g podded fresh peas or
    frozen petit pois, defrosted
6 spring onions, finely sliced
1 Little Gem lettuce, shredded
125g pancetta, cut into cubes
    or thin strips
½ bunch of chives, finely chopped

In a saucepan, melt the butter and add the onion, garlic and thyme. Sweat over a low heat until soft but not coloured. Pour the stock over and bring to the boil then simmer for 5 minutes. Add the defrosted peas and bring back to the boil for 3 minutes, then transfer to a blender or use a stick blender to blend until smooth. Pass through a fine sieve set over a saucepan.

To serve, bring the soup back to the boil then season with salt and pepper to taste. Add all the garnish ingredients, bring to the boil and simmer for a further 3 minutes. Serve in bowls with a drizzle of olive oil.

SNAILS & MEATBALLS MAURICETTE

My parents always made a point of teaching us what the wild and 'tame' lands have to offer depending on the season. When Mother Nature was feeling generous, that abundance was reflected on the family table. Snails and wild mushrooms were of special importance to us and one of my mother's favourite recipes was fresh snails cooked in a vegetable and 'aromatics' stock. She pulled the snails out of their shells to cut off the curled black part at the end, then stuffed them back inside along with Toulouse sausage mince. The snails were then simmered in a tomato, red wine and wild mushroom sauce and served simply with bread and cocktail sticks to pluck them out of their shells. It's a superb dish, which I modified slightly for the opening of Bistrot Bruno Loubet and dedicated to my mother: 'Mauricette snails and meatballs, wild mushrooms Royale'. The dish became an instant classic and has been on the menu since we opened.

Serves 4

4 tbsp olive oil
100g shallots, finely chopped
3 garlic cloves, finely chopped
½ tsp fresh thyme leaves
½ bay leaf
200ml red wine
1 x 227g can chopped tomatoes
150g chestnut mushrooms, quartered
3 Toulouse sausages, casing removed
20 snails, in their shells, black ends
    trimmed
crusty bread, to serve

Herb butter
80g soft butter
1 tbsp chopped tarragon
1 tbsp chopped capers
1 tbsp chopped flat-leaf parsley
1 tbsp chopped chives
1 tsp chopped anchovies
1 tsp Worcestershire sauce
salt and black pepper

In a small saucepan, heat the olive oil, then add the shallots, garlic, thyme and bay leaf and cook over a medium heat for 2 minutes to soften the shallots. Add the red wine, bring to the boil and cook until reduced by half, then add the tomatoes and mushrooms and bring to a gentle simmer. Simmer for another 10–15 minutes, until you have a rich sauce.

Roll the sausage meat into 20 small balls (roughly the size of small cherry tomatoes). Push each snail into its shell, then close the opening with a meatball. Add the snails to the sauce and simmer for 30 minutes.

Place all the ingredients for the herb butter in a small bowl. Mix well, pushing the butter to the sides of the bowl with the back of a spoon. Just before the snails are ready, place the butter in a small pan and heat until foaming.

To serve, spoon the snails and sauce on to plates, then drizzle the foaming butter over and around each serving. Sprinkle over a good grinding of black pepper and serve with fresh crusty bread.

BRUNO'S TIPS

To eat the snails, use cocktail sticks to remove them from their shells. If you don't like the idea of this (or the mess), you can cook the meatballs and the snails without their shells in the sauce, but reduce the cooking time from 30 to 20 minutes.

• • •

Canned snails are okay but freshly cooked snails from a good producer are far better.

WHOLE ARTICHOKE BAKE
WITH GOATS' CHEESE

The artichoke is a type of thistle flower and is in fact eaten when it is still a flower bud. Its flavour is quite unusual: it has a slight metallic taste followed by sweetness. The artichoke has a bad reputation in restaurants as it's difficult to pair with wine, but that has never stopped me enjoying it. I loved it when my mother used to cook whole globe artichokes for dinner – she would only ever buy the large ones from Brittany. Pulling the leaves off one by one and dipping them in mustard vinaigrette was great fun and a build-up of anticipation before reaching the final reward – the heart, filled with runny melted goats' cheese. Delicious!

Serves 4

4 large globe artichokes
240g mature soft goats' cheese
3 tbsp olive oil
salt and black pepper
Family House Vinaigrette
  (see page 236), to serve
toasted baguette slices, to serve

Bring a large casserole of salted water to the boil (don't use an aluminium pan as this may discolour the artichokes).

Prepare the artichokes. Holding the stalk in one hand and the bud in the other, snap the stalk away from the bud. The reason for doing this and not using a knife is that it will pull away any hard fibrous bits running up into the heart. Plunge the artichokes into the boiling water then place a plate over them to keep them completely submerged. Cook for about 15 minutes. Check if they're cooked by pushing a cocktail stick into the bottom of one – it should go in easily. Or, to be sure, pull away a leaf at the bottom – it should come off easily.

Lift the artichokes out of the water and place them in a bowl of iced water for 2 minutes, then remove and place them upside down on a platter to drain. Pull out the centre leaves to create a cavity in the middle (they should come off in one go, as a cone). Use a spoon to scrape out the hairy 'choke' at the cone's base, then reserve the remaining heart.

Cut the cheese into four and place a piece into the cavity of each artichoke, pushing it down with the back of a teaspoon to flatten it. Drizzle over the olive oil and season with a fair amount of pepper. Transfer to a baking dish and place in the oven for 10 minutes or until a sharp knife goes into the centre of the artichoke easily and the cheese is warmed through.

To serve, place each artichoke on a plate with a reserved heart on the side. Serve with the vinaigrette and toasted baguette alongside so that everyone can help themselves.

BRUNO'S TIPS

When buying artichokes, squeeze the base tightly to feel how big the heart is – you need quite large ones for this recipe.

RAW FENNEL & COURGETTE SALAD
WITH HONEY MUSTARD DRESSING

In restaurant kitchens chefs sometimes complicate dishes for commercial reasons or ego. This dish is definitely ego-free and is a favourite summer lunch of mine. Being so simple, the quality of the ingredients is paramount: the fennel must be firm and not too big; the courgettes medium to small and they must feel heavy in your hand; and of course, a good-quality ricotta, preferably organic, is a must.

Serves 4

250g fennel, very finely sliced
    (ideally using a mandoline)
finely grated zest of ½ lemon
1 tbsp lemon juice
200g courgettes, very finely sliced
    (ideally using a mandoline)
½ red onion, very finely sliced
    (ideally using a mandoline)
250g organic ricotta
2 tbsp Greek basil leaves or very small,
    young basil leaves
salt and black pepper

Dressing
1 tbsp honey mustard
3 tbsp olive oil
1 tbsp sherry vinegar
2 tbsp water

Place the fennel in a bowl and add the lemon zest. Season with salt and pepper then add the lemon juice. Toss lightly and set aside.

For the dressing, place all the ingredients in a bowl and mix well using a small whisk until you have an emulsion.

Add the courgettes and red onion to the fennel. When ready to serve, pour over the dressing, toss lightly and place on plates, evenly distributing the colours. Spoon the ricotta over. To finish, add a good crack of pepper and sprinkle over the basil. Serve immediately.

BRUNO'S TIPS

Do not toss the salad and dressing too far ahead – five minutes before serving at the most – to preserve all the textures. Honey mustard is quite easy to find and its mild, sweet flavour will add more depth to your dressing. On hot summer days, the courgette could be replaced by cucumber, sliced slightly thicker, to give the salad crunch.

CHAKCHOUKA WITH MERGUEZ

Chakchouka is a spicy pepper dish from Algeria. It's often served with eggs for breakfast. The first time I experienced it was in Morocco, on a sunny morning while shopping in Casablanca food market. A local friend of mine showed me this little café on a side street and told me that I must try the chakchouka, so of course I did. It was served with piles of bread to dip in the sauce. The smell of the spices coming up from the dish but also pervading the street air is unforgettable.

Serves 4

2 tbsp olive oil, plus extra
   to drizzle
8 merguez sausages, lightly pierced
1 large onion, sliced
4 garlic cloves, sliced
½ red chilli, sliced
½ tsp cumin seeds, toasted and
   finely crushed
2 red peppers, cut into thin strips
1 yellow pepper, cut into thin strips
1 tbsp pomegranate molasses
1 x 227g can chopped tomatoes
1 bay leaf
1 tbsp dried or fresh oregano
pinch of saffron
4 eggs
4 tbsp roughly chopped
   flat-leaf parsley
2 tbsp roughly chopped mint
salt and black pepper
light bread, such as baguette,
   to serve

Preheat the oven to 200°C/fan 180°C/Gas 6.

In a large frying pan, heat the olive oil, then cook the merguez sausages for 2–3 minutes on each side, until cooked through. Lift the merguez out of the pan and set aside.

Add the onion, garlic, chilli and cumin to the pan, and using the merguez cooking oil, fry for 4–5 minutes, stirring from time to time to get a light-brown colour.

Add the peppers and pomegranate molasses and stir well; the mixture will caramelise quickly so keep stirring for a couple of minutes, then add the tomatoes, bay leaf, dried oregano (if using) and saffron and season with salt and pepper. Cover with a lid and leave to simmer for 10 minutes, then add the fresh oregano (if using).

Transfer the mixture to an ovenproof dish and arrange the cooked merguez on top. Make four wells in the pepper mixture using the back of a spoon, then gently break an egg into each well. Bake in the oven for 3–5 minutes, depending on how you like your eggs cooked.

Remove from the oven and sprinkle over the parsley and mint, then drizzle with olive oil. Serve immediately with lots of fresh bread.

BRUNO'S TIPS

As an accompaniment to this dish I like a bit of natural yoghurt, lightly salted and mixed with chopped mint.

POTTED OXTAIL
WITH SAUCE GRIBICHE

During the First World War, the French *poilus* (French infantry soldiers) used to be given tins of corned beef, known as *singe* (monkey meat), as part of their ration – it was the only meat they ate. When I was in the Navy during my National Service, I always wondered why it was called *singe*. The most likely derivation dates back to 1850 and the French general Louis Faidherbe, who was based on the Ivory Coast. Legend has it that he found himself short of supplies so he started to feed his troops monkeys. The name stuck and the tinned beef became tins of *singe*. Don't worry, in this recipe I do not use anything unexpected – only oxtail which, by the way, is utterly delicious. You will need to start preparing the dish at least a day in advance as the oxtail needs time to marinade. It's quite a dense meat so it needs salting a full 24 hours in advance, to allow it time to absorb the seasoning and to tenderise, which also means it will colour more easily during the cooking.

Serves 4

1kg oxtail
150g trimmed leeks, cut into
    large chunks
100g carrots, cut into large chunks
1 onion, cut into large chunks
1 celery stick, trimmed and cut
    into large chunks
1 small bay leaf
60g butter
2 pinches of mace or freshly
    grated nutmeg
1 garlic clove, finely chopped
4 tsp walnut oil
1 tbsp Worcestershire sauce

salt and black pepper
Sauce Gribiche (see page 238),
    to serve
grilled sourdough bread slices,
    to serve

You will need to start preparing this dish the day before you want to serve it (see above). Season the oxtail with salt and pepper then cover with cling film and place in the fridge for 24 hours (no less).

The next day, place the oxtail in a casserole and add enough water to cover the meat by about 3cm. Slowly bring to the boil, then lower the heat to a simmer and skim off any surface scum with a ladle. Add the leek, carrot, onion, celery and bay leaf. Bring back to a simmer and cook for 2½ hours, skimming the surface from time to time.

Carefully lift the cooked oxtail out of the casserole and onto a plate. Strain the liquid through a fine sieve set over a bowl. Transfer the strained stock to a large, shallow frying pan, place over a medium heat and bring to the boil. Reduce the heat and simmer for about 30 minutes, until you have only about 100ml left.

In a saucepan, heat the butter until foaming. Remove from the heat then add the mace, garlic, walnut oil and the 100ml of reduced stock. Pour it all into a bowl set inside a larger bowl of iced water. Whisk from time to time until the mixture is cold and has a custard consistency.

Meanwhile, pick the meat from the oxtail bone and add it to the cooled butter mixture along with the Worcestershire sauce. Mix well with a spoon so that everything binds well – it should be like soft rillettes. Divide the mixture between four ramekins and place in the fridge for a minimum of 20 minutes so that it starts to set.

To serve, remove the ramekins from the fridge and allow the mixture to come back to room temperature (i.e. soften up a bit so that it is not firm and set), then serve with the Sauce Gribiche and grilled sourdough.

BRUNO'S TIPS

This dish can be made up to three days ahead and stored in the fridge. To give an extra depth of flavour, cut the onions into thick slices and fry them in a dry frying pan until deep brown on each side then add them to the casserole as described above.

CRAB, CORN, GINGER & CHILLI RISOTTO

A friend of mine used to say: 'When I eat saffron risotto, it reminds me of my beloved Lombardy and sunshine on a plate!' – very romantic. Of course, most Italians will tell you the risotto their mother used to cook for them is the best they've ever had and often refer to a secret ingredient, pot or technique. Let's get back to reality; there are just three important steps to follow when making risotto. First, tossing the rice with the onions until the rice turns opaque ensures that the rice is coated in the oil and so the grains will be less likely to stick together. Second, gradually adding the liquids – wine and stock or water – so the rice can absorb them before more is added, results in the release of starch, which gives the risotto its creamy texture. Third, enriching the risotto with butter then adding an acid like lemon juice or vinegar pushes the other flavours forward and makes the dish even tastier. The Asian flavour of this recipe might make a legion of 'mamas' raise their eyebrows but in my opinion it tastes great. I'll let you judge for yourself!

Serves 4

2 fresh corn cobs
800ml fish stock
100g butter
150g onions (approx. 1 large),
    finely chopped
1 garlic clove, finely chopped
1 tsp finely sliced red chilli
300g arborio rice
100ml dry white wine
6 spring onions, finely sliced
1 tsp finely chopped fresh root ginger
160g picked white and brown crabmeat
    (see Bruno's Tips)
1 tsp lemon juice
salt and black pepper

Slice the corn kernels from one cob, and place in a saucepan with 300ml of the fish stock. Bring to the boil then lower the heat, cover with a lid and simmer for 20 minutes. Remove from the heat and blend until as smooth as possible, then pass through a fine sieve, pushing the solids down to extract as much of the liquid as possible. Discard the solids and set the stock aside.

Cut the corn kernels from the other cob. In a frying pan, heat 60g of the butter until foaming, then add the onions, garlic and chilli and cook over a medium heat until the onions soften but do not brown – about 3–4 minutes – then add the rice. Mix well with a wooden spoon and cook for 3 minutes, until the rice turns a pearly opaque colour. Add the wine and continue cooking for another minute. Add the corn kernels and enough stock to reach the level of the rice, then stir constantly until most of the liquid has been absorbed. Repeat until all the stock has been used – the total cooking time should be between 15 and 18 minutes but no more. Add the spring onion, ginger, crab, lemon juice and remaining butter. Stir well for 1 minute, then check the seasoning. Serve immediately.

BRUNO'S TIPS

Buy fresh, young corn on the cob. The corn grains should not be big and yellow but medium to small and pale yellow to creamy white.

• • •

Although white crabmeat is often considered the greater delicacy, many shops sell picked crab that contains a mixture of the white and brown meat. Do not be suspicious of it, the brown meat will give the risotto an orangey brown colour and depth of flavour.

GRILLED & SMOKED AUBERGINES
WITH CREAMED CITRUS DRESSING, POMEGRANATE & FRESH MINT

Over the years, the aubergine has become one of my favourite vegetables; I love its taste but also its creamy texture. There are many varieties of aubergine and their cooking time changes accordingly, but the most common is the purple one I use in this recipe. I use two cooking processes: chargrilling but also flaming the aubergine, which helps to enhance its smoky flavour. This smokiness will complement any fish or meat cooked on the barbecue or you could serve this dish on its own as a starter.

Serves 4

3 aubergines
juice of ½ lemon
1 tbsp tahini
3 tbsp olive oil, plus extra to cook
    the aubergines
2 tbsp finely sliced mint
2 tbsp pomegranate seeds
salt and black pepper

Dressing
1 tbsp lime juice
3 tbsp orange juice
4 tbsp olive oil
½ tsp sugar
2 tbsp natural yoghurt
1 egg yolk

Cook one of the aubergines by placing it on an open gas flame, turning it frequently with tongs, until blackened all over. This should take around 5 minutes. Wrap in foil and leave to cool.

Cut the other two aubergines in half lengthways then slice off a thin length on the skin side so that they can sit flat. Season with salt and pepper and set aside.

In the meantime, open the foil, and cut the flamed aubergine in two. Scoop out the smoky flesh. Place this flesh in a food processor with the lemon juice, tahini and olive oil. Season then process to a fine purée. Transfer to a bowl and set aside.

Brush the aubergine halves with a little olive oil and grill on a cast-iron griddle set over a high heat or a hot barbecue for about 2–3 minutes on each side, turning them so that you end up with griddle marks in a criss-cross pattern.

Meanwhile, prepare the dressing. Place all the ingredients in a blender or use a stick blender to process until smooth and creamy.

To serve, spoon the aubergine purée on to a serving dish and spread out a little. Place the chargrilled aubergines on top, then drizzle over the dressing and sprinkle with the mint and pomegranate seeds. Add extra olive oil if you like.

BRUNO'S TIPS

Fresh aubergines should feel heavy in your hand, you don't want the spongy ones.

• • •

After chargrilling the aubergines, I suggest you wrap them in cling film until they cool down to make sure they are nice and soft in the middle.

GOATS' CHEESE & SOFT GREENS QUICHE

Quiches often get a bad rap, usually because they are cooked too quickly at high temperatures or for too long, which results in an eggy, dry filling with holes in it. If cooked properly, quiches will have a delicate, velvety custard texture with a crisp golden crust. In this recipe, goats' cheese adds flavour and lots of greens makes it reasonably healthy. I usually serve this quiche with a heritage tomato salad.

Serves 8

Pastry
240g plain flour
2 pinches of salt
1 tsp dried Provençal herbs
180g unsalted butter, diced
60ml water

Filling
2 bok choi, leaves separated, stalks cut
*   into 2cm pieces*
200g broccoli tops
4 tsp olive oil
100g spinach
320ml double cream
2 eggs, plus 4 egg yolks
2 pinches of freshly grated nutmeg
2 tbsp basil pesto
250g semi-hard goats' cheese, crumbled
salt and black pepper

BRUNO'S TIPS

After blind baking, brush the inside of the pastry case with an egg yolk and place in the oven for 30 seconds before filling it; this will create an impermeable barrier and the pastry will be more crispy.

For the pastry, place the flour on a work surface then make a well in the middle. Sprinkle the salt and herbs all over, then put the diced butter into the well and bring the flour into the centre. Using the tips of your fingers, work the flour into the butter until partly combined. Make another well in the centre, then pour in the water. Mix quickly then knead it for a few moments, just until it comes together. The dough will be quite lumpy. Make a ball with the dough, then flatten it a bit. Wrap in cling film and chill for 30 minutes.

Preheat the oven to 220°C/fan 200°C/Gas 7. Lightly grease a 28cm tart tin. When ready, lightly flour a work surface and roll out the pastry. Check the size by turning the tart tin upside down on top of the pastry. The diameter of the pastry should be 5cm bigger than the dish. Roll the pastry gently on to the rolling pin then unroll it over the tin. Push the pastry into the edges of the tin, pressing against the sides with your thumbs. Let the pastry hang over the edge of the tin, then cut off the overhang leaving just 1cm. Place in the freezer for 10 minutes, then cover with greaseproof paper and fill the inside with baking beans or dried beans.

Bake for 15 minutes, then remove the beans and paper and bake for a further 5 minutes, until golden and crisp. Remove from the oven and set aside. Reduce the oven setting to 195°C/fan 175°C/Gas 5½.

Blanch the bok choi in salted boiling water for 30 seconds. Drain and refresh in iced water. Repeat with the broccoli tops. Drain again then pat dry. Heat the olive oil in a large casserole or frying pan, add the spinach, bok choi and broccoli. Cook until the spinach is completely wilted, then squeeze out the excess water and set aside.

In a mixing bowl, combine the cream, eggs and yolks, nutmeg, pesto and salt and pepper. Mix well with a whisk. Spread the greens in the pastry case, add the crumbled cheese, then fill with the cream mixture. Bake in the oven for about 25 minutes, until set and golden brown on top. Rest the quiche for at least 5 minutes before slicing as it will cut more cleanly.

SPRING OEUFS EN GELÉE

Oeufs en gelée is a common French speciality of a soft-boiled or poached egg set inside a meat-flavoured jelly. They are generally found in charcuterie shops all over France. My mother sometimes used to make them with the leftovers from a boiling fowl (*poule au pot*), diced vegetables and tarragon. Sometimes she would simply buy them from the *charcutier* on the way to a picnic.

Serves 6

50g fresh peas
60g carrots, diced
60g fennel, diced
50g tomatoes, peeled (optional) and diced
4 tbsp soy sauce
1 tsp tarragon
6 small eggs (see Bruno's Tips)
salt and black pepper
mixed salad leaves, to serve

Jelly
500g chicken necks
1 pig's trotter
200g carrots
200g onions (approx. 2 medium)
150g celery
150g leeks
2 garlic cloves
1 small bay leaf
5 thyme sprigs
4 tbsp crushed mixed peppercorns
3 egg whites
6 ice cubes, crushed
salt

Start by preparing the jelly. Place the chicken necks and pig's trotter in a casserole with two litres of cold water. Add three pinches of salt and bring to the boil. Skim the surface and add the remaining jelly ingredients, except the egg whites and ice cubes, then lower the heat to a gentle simmer. Partly cover the pan with a lid and cook for 2 hours, then pass through a fine sieve. Bring the strained bouillon back to the boil, then one by one, cook the peas, carrots, fennel and tomatoes until tender, then remove and set aside. Bring the bouillon back to the boil.

In a small bowl, whisk the egg whites for 10 seconds then add the crushed ice cubes. Pour the egg whites into the bouillon, stirring continuously. Lower the heat to medium and wait for a white cake to form at the top of the bouillon. Leave to simmer for 5 minutes then line a sieve with a muslin and pass the bouillon through the cloth into a clean pan.

Boil the clear bouillon until it has reduced to 600ml, then add the soy sauce and tarragon. Place the bouillon in a bowl set inside a larger bowl of iced water.

Get ready six ramekins about 8cm in diameter and 5cm deep. Pour 1cm of chilled bouillon into each ramekin and place in the fridge for about 15 minutes to set.

Meanwhile, place the eggs in a pan, cover with cold water and bring to the boil. Boil for 4 minutes, then remove and place in cold water to stop them cooking.

Once cool enough to handle, peel the eggs and place one in the centre of each ramekin, then pour over the jelly. Divide the diced vegetables between the moulds and transfer to the fridge to set (up to 4 hours).

To serve, turn the eggs out of their moulds by pushing the side of the jelly to create an air pocket – turn them out upside down onto serving plates and serve with salad leaves.

BRUNO'S TIPS

You really do need to buy small eggs for this recipe otherwise they will be too large for the ramekins and won't be fully covered by the jelly.

. . .

I suggest you make the consommé a few days before or even a week ahead and freeze so it will be easy to complete the dish on the day.

SLOW-BAKED ONIONS
IN THEIR SKINS
WITH CHEDDAR & SAGE

Weeping won't be a problem with this recipe as you do not need to peel the onions. The onions are baked in their skins, which act as a protective mould for the juicy flesh. The natural moisture will help the cooking process and preserve the flavour. The addition of mature Cheddar and sage makes it a fabulous dish, which usually surprises around the table. A soft-boiled egg cut in half for each person, lots of 'soldiers' and a bowl of mixed salad leaves in a walnut dressing will round off a comforting supper.

Serves 6

6 onions
120g butter
240g mature Cheddar
1 tbsp sage leaves, finely chopped
¼ tsp freshly grated nutmeg
salt and black pepper
dressed mixed salad, to serve

Preheat the oven to 200°C/fan 180°C/ Gas 6.

Cut the root at the base of the onions as low as possible with a sharp knife, leaving the layers attached to the base. Make an incision 2.5cm down from the top of the onions all around the circumference, then prick them with a fork all over. Wrap each onion in a layer of foil and season with salt and pepper before you close it tightly.

Place in a roasting tin with 500ml of water and bake in the oven for about 1 hour or until a sharp knife goes in easily. Lower the oven setting to 170°C/fan 150°C/Gas 3½.

Open the foil then let the onions cool. While the onions are cooling, place the butter in a small saucepan and heat gently until it starts to brown, then remove from the heat.

When cool enough to handle, take the onions out of the foil and cut off the tops where you made the previous incisions and set them aside. Carefully spoon out the flesh (it should be completely soft), leaving the three outer layers. Place the flesh on a chopping board and chop into small pieces, then place in a mixing bowl.

Add the Cheddar, browned butter, sage and nutmeg. Spoon the mixture back into the onion shells and replace the tops. Place on a baking sheet and return to the oven for about 10 minutes, until heated through.

Serve with mixed leaves in a French dressing.

BRUNO'S TIPS

If you're feeling 'grand' or want to give somebody the VIP treatment, shave some fresh truffle over the onions and you will have a dish fit for a king!

GORGONZOLA, WALNUT & BACON STUFFED MUSHROOMS

We often have a large Sunday lunch so dinner is usually light. This dish came about one evening when I didn't have much time to cook and there was something unmissable on TV, so I threw together what was left in the larder and the fridge. The dish is so easy to prepare and the mushrooms cook in a very short time. Serve it with a bowl of mixed leaf and rocket salad and it's a perfect 30-minute dinner.

Serves 4

4 large flat open mushrooms
2 slices of wholemeal bread,
*   cut into tiny pieces*
40g walnuts, roughly chopped
1 tbsp chopped flat-leaf parsley
120g Gorgonzola cheese
1 tbsp basil pesto
½ tsp Dijon mustard
3 tbsp olive oil
200g smoked streaky bacon,
*   cut into small dice or strips*
½ tsp horseradish cream
mixed leaf and rocket salad,
*   to serve*

Preheat the oven to 220°C/fan 200°C/ Gas 7.

Pull off the mushroom stalks, chop them finely and place in a mixing bowl. Add the bread to the bowl along with the walnuts, parsley, Gorgonzola, pesto and mustard. Add 1 tablespoon of the olive oil.

Heat the remaining olive oil in a small frying pan and fry the bacon until lightly coloured. Drain the bacon over a container to reserve the fat. Add the bacon to the bowl along with the horseradish cream and mix well with a spoon until you get a kind of stuffing. Divide the stuffing between the mushroom caps, filling the whole cavity. Place the mushrooms in a baking dish, then spoon some of the reserved oil from the bacon over them (this is optional, depending on how healthy you want to be!). Bake in the oven for about 6 minutes, until the topping is golden and the cheese is bubbling.

Place the mushrooms on serving plates, with the juices spooned over, and the salad.

BRUNO'S TIPS

The bacon could be replaced with leftover roast chicken or sausages.

PEA PANCAKES & POACHED EGG WITH BALSAMIC SYRUP

I love this dish because it is not what you expect from a pancake and you can adapt it to the occasion. For breakfast, you could add some crispy bacon or a slice of smoked salmon, or to serve it as a vegetarian main course sprinkle over a bit of crumbled feta cheese.

Serves 6

2 tbsp olive oil, plus extra to serve
75g butter
6 eggs
1–2 tbsp balsamic syrup
3 tbsp chopped chives
100g pea shoots
white wine vinegar,
    for poaching the eggs

Pancakes
500g frozen petit pois
50g butter
3 tbsp cornflour
2 eggs, separated
salt and black pepper

For the pancakes, cook the peas in boiling salted water for a few minutes, until tender, then drain in a colander.

Place the butter in a small non-stick frying pan over a medium heat and cook until light brown, then remove from the heat.

Place the peas in a food processor with the cornflour, egg yolks, brown butter and seasoning and process to make a fairly smooth purée, then transfer to a bowl. Whisk the egg whites until stiff peaks form then gently fold into the pea mixture.

Heat a large non-stick frying pan with 1 tablespoon of olive oil and half of the butter. When the butter starts to foam, use half the pea mixture to ladle three pancakes into the pan. Cook them until golden on each side. Keep warm in a low oven (120°C/fan 100°C/Gas ½). Repeat with the remaining oil, butter and batter. Keep warm while you poach the eggs.

Bring a large saucepan of salted water to a gentle simmer, then add 3 tablespoons of white wine vinegar. Have ready a tray covered with a hot damp tea towel that has been wrung out.

Carefully break the eggs into little cups then slowly pour each one into the simmering water, letting them slide to the sides of the pan. Leave to simmer for a few minutes, until the whites have set. Remove with a slotted spoon and place on the hot tea towel – doing this will make it easier to transfer the eggs to the serving plates without breaking them. Gently fold over the tea towel to cover the eggs and keep them hot.

To serve, place a pancake in the middle of each serving plate and top with a poached egg. Drizzle over the balsamic syrup then the olive oil and sprinkle over the chives and pea shoots.

BRUNO'S TIPS

If you want to prepare the pancakes in advance, cook them up to one hour before serving then sandwich them between two sheets of buttered greaseproof paper. Reheat by spraying them with water and placing in an oven set at 200°C/fan 180°C/Gas 6 for 3 minutes before serving.

• • •

At home I like to serve this dish with some Boursin cheese alongside.

LOBSTER SALAD
« WATEGO »

Watego Beach is in Byron Bay, Australia. To my mind it is one of the most strikingly beautiful places on earth, oozing charm. One Boxing Day lunch we sat on the grass between the famous 'Rae's on Watego' restaurant and the beach to enjoy a lobster salad I put together for the occasion, with a bottle of Viognier. The moment was so magical that we decided to make it a regular event every Boxing Day when we lived in Australia and the salad now appears on my restaurant menu. This recipe sounds glamorous but is actually quite simple; the hardest part is finding a dream beach that matches Watego! If your lobster has eggs you can add them to the salad.

Serves 4

2 live lobsters, about 500g each
2 jasmine teabags
2 small, firm courgettes, trimmed and
    cut into fine ribbons using a
    mandoline or peeler
1 fennel bulb, trimmed and finely sliced
1 mango, peeled and finely sliced
4 spring onions, finely sliced
6 mint leaves, finely sliced
8 basil leaves, finely sliced
½ tsp finely sliced chilli
salt

Dressing
2 tbsp olive oil
1 tbsp sesame oil
1 tbsp lime juice
1 tsp clear honey
⅓ tsp finely grated fresh root ginger

Place the lobsters in the freezer for 2 hours to make them unconscious. Bring 3 litres of water to the boil in a large, deep pan with 2 tablespoons of salt. When boiling, plunge the lobsters inside and push them down with a spoon to immerse them completely. Add the teabags, lower the heat to a simmer and cook for about 5 minutes or until the lobster shells have turned a deep red. Remove the pan from the heat and leave the lobsters to rest in the water for 2 minutes, then lift the lobsters out of the water and plunge them into iced water for 3 minutes. Remove to a plate and set aside.

Put the courgettes, fennel, mango, spring onions, mint, basil and chilli in a bowl and season with salt.

For the dressing, place all the ingredients in a small bowl and whisk well to combine.

Place the lobsters on a tea towel on a work surface. Cut off the claws, then crack the shell of the body and tail. Pull off the tail and peel like a prawn, then cut the body in half. Discard the pale stomach sac and feathery gills then remove all the meat from the bodies. Remove the dark intestinal thread that runs down the tail flesh. Put the claws on a chopping board and crack them open with the back of a heavy knife and extract the meat. Pick out the leg meat. Cut the thick lobster meat into medallions.

Add the dressing to the salad and toss gently with two spoons. Divide between serving plates, top with the lobster and serve.

BRUNO'S TIPS

Reserve the lobster shells and use them to make a stock or bisque. They can be frozen for up to 1 month.

• • •

If the mango is not ripe enough, I suggest you slice it and place it on a dish, drizzle with lime juice, sprinkle over a little sugar and leave to marinate for 30 minutes – this will sweeten and soften it.

PATES & TERRINES

I have very fond memories of going fishing with my father: it was one of the rare moments when I could ask him questions and get answers. I also loved the lunch break. Early in the morning, before we set off, my father would cut a large piece of Pyrenees cheese and wrap it in a tea towel, then on the way he would stop at the baker to buy some fresh crusty bread and at the charcuterie for a thick slice of pâté. It's funny how small moments from your childhood can remain pin-sharp in your memory. When I remember our fishing trips, two things come to my mind: the dialogue with my father and eating this wonderful pâté. I can clearly see the blade of my father's Opinel knife cutting through the coarse farce (literally a meat stuffing) spiked with chunks of pink meat and soft lard, and sharing it with my brother. It was one of the best moments of my life and one that I still cherish.

Like sauces, a pâté or terrine can be a sophisticated concoction, demanding great skill and knowledge. However, a good basic pâté is not difficult to make and brings great pleasure. The difference between a pâté and a terrine is that a pâté consists of a farce cooked in a mould called a terrine – it can be smooth or coarse. A terrine is more complex, with alternate layers of farce and pieces of meat or dried fruits, mushrooms etc., again cooked in a terrine.

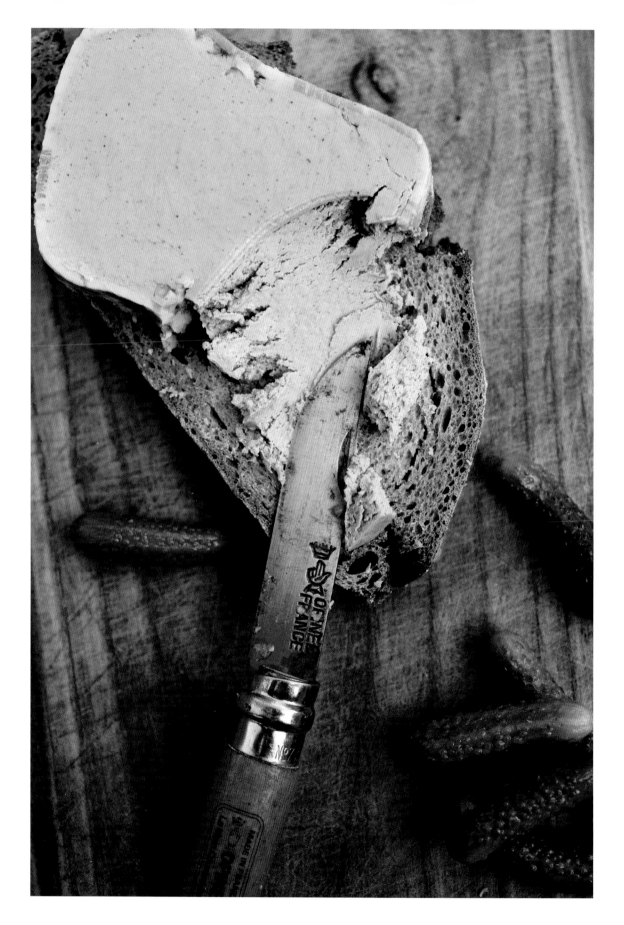

SMOOTH CHICKEN LIVER PATE

Serves 10–12

500g butter
500g chicken livers, cleaned,
    dried and trimmed
5 eggs
5 tsp salt
½ tsp freshly ground black pepper
½ tsp ground allspice
12 prosciutto slices

Flavouring
100g shallots, peeled and finely sliced
50ml Port
50ml Madeira
25ml brandy
3 garlic cloves
3 sprigs fresh thyme

Start by preparing the flavouring. Place all the ingredients in a saucepan, bring to a gentle simmer and simmer until the shallots are completely soft. You might need to add a bit of water from time to time but you should be left with about 2 tablespoons of liquid.

Melt the butter slowly over a gentle heat so that it does not rise in temperature too much. Place the flavouring in a blender with a third of the butter and blitz until puréed and smooth. Then add the chicken livers, eggs, salt, pepper and allspice. Blitz again, then pour in the remaining butter and blitz until the mixture becomes liquid, smooth and pinkish in colour. Pour into a bowl, cover with cling film and place in the fridge for 6 hours to set.

Preheat the oven to 120°C/fan 100°C/ Gas ½. Line a 1.1 litre terrine mould (about 28cm x 11cm x 7.5cm) with foil, leaving at least a 10cm overhang of foil. Line with the prosciutto slices so that they overlap to cover the base and sides and leave an overhang. Spoon the liver mixture inside, then fold the prosciutto over to encase the mixture. Fold over the foil then cover with the lid.

Place the terrine in a roasting tin and pour in enough hot water to come two–thirds of the way up the sides of the mould. Bake in the oven for 1¼ hours or until a probe inserted into the centre of the pâté reaches 70°C or insert a metal skewer and hold it there for 5 seconds; it should feel piping hot. Once it has reached 70°C, cook for a further 5 minutes. Remove from the oven and allow to cool completely. Ideally you should leave it for at least 24 hours before serving as this improves the flavour.

To turn the terrine out of its mould, briefly dip the terrine in hot water, shake to loosen then turn out on to a serving plate.

COUNTRY-STYLE PATE

Instead of a terrine, I use a cast-iron cocotte for this pâté to give it an even more traditional look.

Serves 10–12

450g pork back fat
200g chicken livers, cleaned, dried
    and trimmed
5 tsp salt
½ tsp freshly ground black pepper
300g lean pork belly, placed in the
    freezer for 20 minutes
400g pork neck, placed in the freezer
    for 20 minutes
½ a nutmeg, grated
3 garlic cloves
1 tbsp chopped tarragon
50ml white wine
3 tbsp brandy
½ tbsp fresh thyme leaves
4 tbsp dried breadcrumbs
2 eggs
100g caul fat, soaked in cold water for
    1 hour then washed thoroughly (see
    Bruno's Tips, page 51), or sliced
    streaky bacon

Preheat the oven to 130°C/fan 110°C/ Gas ¾.

Place 350g of the back fat in a food processor and process until completely smooth, then add the chicken livers and purée again until liquid. Season with the salt and pepper.

On a chopping board, chop the pork belly and neck to a coarse mince (about 5mm cubes or use the large blade of an electric mincer if you have one) then spread them out on a tray. Season with nutmeg.

Place all the remaining ingredients except the caul fat in a bowl. Using disposable plastic gloves, mix the farce well until the mixture is completely bound together. Line a 1.1 litre terrine mould (about 28cm x 11cm x 7.5cm) or cast-iron oval cocotte (about 20cm x 15cm x 8cm) with foil, leaving at least a 10cm overhang of foil.

Line with the caul fat or bacon. If using bacon, make sure that the slices overlap to cover the base and sides and leave an overhang. Pack the farce into the terrine, pressing it down with a fork. Fold over the overhanging caul fat or bacon then the foil, then cover with the lid.

Bake in the oven for 1 hour 20 minutes or until a probe inserted into the centre of the pâté reaches 70°C or insert a metal skewer and hold it there for 5 seconds; it should be piping hot. Once it has reached 70°C, cook for a further 5 minutes. Remove from the oven and allow to cool completely. Ideally you should leave it for at least 24 hours before serving as this improves the flavour.

To turn the terrine out of its mould, briefly dip the terrine in hot water, shake to loosen then turn out. (Pictured on page 50, top right.)

CHICKEN TERRINE NICOISE-STYLE

Serves 10–12

200g pork back fat

250g unsmoked streaky bacon

300g boneless chicken thighs,
    placed in the freezer for 20 minutes

200g pork belly, placed in the freezer
    for 20 minutes

350g chicken breasts, without skin,
    placed in the freezer for 20 minutes

celery salt, to taste

½ freshly ground black pepper

4 garlic cloves

1 tbsp chopped marjoram

120g semi-dried tomatoes,
    cut into 5mm slices

100g pitted black olives, halved

1 whole egg

12 thin, mild pancetta slices

Preheat the oven to 150°C/fan 130°C/Gas 2.

Purée the pork fat in a food processor until fine. Process the bacon in the food processor as well, but not too fine.

On a chopping board, chop the chicken thighs and pork belly until each is a coarse mince. Cut the chicken breast into 1.5cm cubes. Lay all the meats out on a large, flat surface and season with the celery salt and freshly ground black pepper. Place in a large bowl and add all the remaining ingredients, except the pancetta slices.

Using disposable plastic gloves, mix the farce well until the mixture is completely bound together. Line a 1.1-litre terrine mould (about 28cm x 11cm x 7.5cm) with foil, leaving at least a 10cm overhang of foil. Line with the pancetta slices so that they overlap to cover the base and sides and leave an overhang. Pack the farce into the terrine, pressing it down with a fork. Cover the top with any remaining pancetta, then fold over the overhang to wrap tightly and cover with the lid. Place the terrine in a roasting tin and pour in enough hot water to come two–thirds of the way up the sides of the mould. Bake in the oven for 1–1½ hours or until a probe inserted into the centre of the terrine reaches 80°C. Once it has reached 80°C cook for a further 5 minutes.

When cooked, place the terrine in a container with cold water and ice cubes around it to cool it as quickly as possible. Once cool, place in the fridge to set for 24 hours.

To turn the terrine out of its mould, briefly dip the terrine in hot water, shake to loosen then turn out. (Pictured on page 50, top left.)

BRUNO'S TIPS

For terrine and pâté farces, it is better to chop the meat while it is very cold with a heavy knife rather than using the ready-minced meat, which is why I've suggested placing your meat in the freezer for 20 minutes before chopping it. It can take some time but it will give a much better texture to the end result.

. . .

When you place the farce in the mould, add it a little at a time, pushing it down well with a fork before adding more, to avoid having cavities in the terrine.

. . .

Caul fat is the fatty membrane that encases the inner organs of pigs, cows and sheep. It looks like a fat white lace. It's naturally sticky so is great for wrapping meat, and as it cooks, the fat melts, keeping the meat inside it moist. You can buy it from your butcher but you will need to pre-order it. Clean it thoroughly before using by soaking it in water and a splash of vinegar for an hour then rinsing well.

. . .

It's a good idea to invest in an electronic food thermometer (probe) to check the cooking level at the centre of the terrine. It should reach 70°C for meat terrines (or 80°C for chicken-based terrines) and remain at that temperature for 5 minutes. This clever tool will become indispensable in your kitchen.

. . .

Unfortunately pâtés do have a high fat content and this is difficult to avoid otherwise the pâté will be dry. Eat salad and drink red wine with it; that is my argument anyway!

. . .

The pâtés and terrines are cooked in a hot water bath, which ensures that they are cooked gently and evenly throughout because the heat is conducted uniformly.

Opposite, clockwise from bottom:
Smooth Chicken Liver Pâté, Chicken Terrine Niçoise-style,
Country-style Pâté

PISSALADIERE WITH MARINATED SARDINE FILLETS

Pissaladière is a kind of pizza from Nice on the Côte d'Azur. It is very popular on restaurant menus but also as street food sold in vans, and of course in many households. The bread dough base is covered with a layer of melting, caramelised onions, anchovies and olives.

The name *pissaladière* comes from the Provençal word *pissalat*, which is a paste made of anchovies but also salted sardines, so it seemed only natural to me to add the marinated sardines to my version. I also love the contrast between the cooked salted anchovies and the soft sea flavour of the fresh sardines. This is great with a bit of rocket salad and curly endive on the top. And perhaps a nice glass of Bandol rosé to remind me of my holiday in Nice?

Serves 4

800g onions, sliced
3 garlic cloves, crushed and chopped
1 tsp dried Provençal herbs
50ml olive oil
8 anchovy fillets, in olive oil
8 black olives, stoned and halved
20 small basil leaves
mixed leaf salad dressed in olive oil
    and lemon, to serve
salt

Dough
10g fresh yeast
150ml lukewarm water
250g strong white flour, plus extra
    for dusting
2 pinches of sugar
2 tbsp olive oil
1 tsp salt

Marinated sardines
6 medium sardine fillets
juice of 1 lemon
3 tbsp olive oil
1 tbsp baby capers
salt and black pepper

First, marinate the sardines. Pour the lemon juice into a shallow dish. Season the sardines on both sides then dip them one by one in the lemon juice. Place on a plate and pour over the remaining juice, then drizzle with the olive oil. Add the capers. Cover with cling film and leave to marinate for at least two hours.

Place the onions in a bowl with a bit of salt, the garlic and the Provençal herbs. Mix well with your hands then squeeze the onions a little – this will help extract the water and make the onions cook quickly. Place the onions in a pan with the olive oil, cover with a lid and cook them over a medium heat to soften them. Cook for about 8 minutes, then remove the lid and increase the heat to high.

Continue to cook, stirring from time to time, so that the onions are coloured evenly. It should take about 10–12 minutes for the onions to become well caramelised and for all the liquid to have evaporated.

Preheat the oven to 200°C/fan 180°C/Gas 6. Line a baking sheet with non-stick baking paper.

Make the dough. Dissolve the yeast in a small bowl with half the lukewarm water. Add three tablespoons of the flour and the sugar. Whisk well then cover tightly with cling film and transfer to a warm place to rise for about 10 minutes. The mixture should double in volume.

Place the yeast mixture and all the remaining dough ingredients in a bowl or the bowl of an electric mixer.

If using a mixer, use the paddle attachment and mix well for 3 minutes. If kneading by hand, place the dough on a lightly floured work surface and knead the dough for 6–8 minutes, until soft and stretchy, then return to the bowl. Cover with a damp tea towel and transfer to a warm place for about 15 minutes to double in volume.

Knead the dough for 30 seconds, then roll the dough out to a 22cm-diameter circle. Transfer to the prepared baking sheet. Spread the onions over the dough, then lay the anchovies evenly around the dough, as if they were the hands of a clock face, then place an olive into the gaps between the anchovies. Bake for about 10 minutes or until the dough is golden and crisp on the bottom and the top is golden brown.

Remove from the oven and arrange the drained sardines over the top. Scatter over the basil leaves. Slice the pissaladière at the table, served with the dressed mixed salad.

BRUNO'S TIPS

If you don't fancy the idea of the marinated sardines then either add seasoned sardines after 8 minutes of cooking for the remaining time, or simply omit them.

SOUSED MACKEREL
& WASABI POTATO SALAD

For me, mackerel is a great mystery. Why on earth has this fantastic fish been so neglected for so long? Not only is the oily flesh delicious, but the patterns of its silver and green camouflaged skin look so attractive. Mackerel can only be eaten extremely fresh or the flavour can deteriorate and become too strong. Fortunately, fish can now be transported around so quickly that this revered fish is making a comeback. Do take full advantage of this cheap, once unsung hero!

Serves 4

4 mackerel fillets
100ml dry white wine
1 tbsp clear honey
40g shallots
½ tsp lemon thyme leaves
1 bay leaf
50ml cider vinegar
2 tbsp olive oil
350g new potatoes, halved if large
4 tbsp mayonnaise
2 tsp wasabi paste
1 tbsp finely sliced green chilli
6 spring onions, finely sliced
1 Granny Smith apple, cored
*   and finely sliced*
1 handful of coriander leaves
salt and black pepper

Place the mackerel fillets in a shallow dish that fits them snugly. Season the fillets with salt and pepper on both sides then leave to marinate in the fridge for 15 minutes.

Meanwhile, pour the wine into a small saucepan, add the honey, shallots, thyme and bay leaf. Bring to the boil then cover with a lid and remove from the heat. Leave for 15 minutes for the flavours to infuse. Bring the marinade back to the boil, add the vinegar then pour over the fish. Pour over the olive oil, then cover tightly with cling film and place in the fridge for at least 3 hours.

Meanwhile, place the new potatoes in a pan, cover with water, bring to boil, then simmer for 8–10 minutes, until tender. Drain and set aside to cool.

When the mackerel is ready, mix the mayonnaise in a bowl with the wasabi, green chilli and spring onions, then add the potatoes and apple and mix well again.

To serve, place the mackerel on a chopping board. Slice each fillet at a 45° angle, then slide the blade underneath the fillet and transfer to a serving plate. Repeat with the other fillets then spoon the potatoes on to each plate.

Sprinkle over the coriander. Just before serving, spoon some of the marinade over each plate.

BRUNO'S TIPS

When heating the marinade, do not use an aluminum or copper pan as the acid mix will have an abrasive effect on the pan. Use a stainless-steel, glass or earthenware pan.

SPICED SALMON TARTARE

Salmon tartare is often found on bistrot menus in France but in my opinion is often spoilt and a disappointment. The fish should just be lightly cured (i.e. not in too much salt) and it should have a raw texture rather than feel slimy as if it's starting to cook.

In this recipe the spicy, sweet and sour dressing of North African flavours gives the dish plenty of character and makes it a winner for all seasons. I've provided two alternative garnishes, one that will be more appropriate for autumn and winter and another for spring and summer.

You need to ensure you cut very thin slices of bread for this dish; a thick piece of bread doesn't work as it will detract from the delicate texture of the dish.

Serves 4

400g salmon fillet, with skin

Marinade
2 tbsp Maldon sea salt
1 tsp sugar
⅓ tsp fennel seeds
grated zest of ¼ lemon
freshly ground black pepper

Dressing
juice of ½ lemon
1 tbsp clear honey
½ tsp cumin seeds, toasted then ground
⅓ tsp finely grated fresh root ginger
1 tbsp pomegranate molasses
½ tsp harissa

Autumn/winter garnish
1 tbsp pomegranate seeds
1 tbsp finely chopped coriander
*2 tbsp mint leaves, cut into two
   or three pieces*

Spring/summer garnish
16 fresh breakfast radishes
a handful of pea shoots
2 tbsp finely chopped chives

The night before you wish to serve the dish, place the salmon fillets, skin-side down, on a large sheet of foil. Sprinkle the ingredients for the marinade evenly over the fish, making sure the mixture is slightly more generous on the thickest part of the fillet. Close the foil to make a parcel, then place the parcel on a plate, and cover it with another plate to weigh it down. Place in the fridge for at least 12 hours.

The next day, make the dressing by whisking all the ingredients in a bowl. Open the salmon parcel and rinse the fillet under cold running water. Pat dry then cut away the skin. Cut the salmon into slices, about 7mm thick, then cut these into 7mm strips and cut across them to make small dice that are as regular as possible.

Divide the salmon between four serving plates, spreading it around. Arrange the appropriate garnish around the plate, then carefully drizzle the dressing over the plates.

BRUNO'S TIPS

Do not purchase your fish ahead of time; buy it on the day you are going to cure it to make sure it is as fresh as possible.

ASPARAGUS ROASTED WITH MEAT JUS

As a child, I used to spend many hours in our vegetable garden. For my school friends, this was unusual, bizarre even, but for me it was my pride and joy and my favourite playground. This was where I could use my imagination. We used to have an asparagus bed made up of two 10m rows topped with a mound of earth. The ground was quite sandy and when watered a crust would form on top. I realised that if the rows were watered at night, by morning little cracks would have appeared indicating the presence of a 'rocket'. The 'rocket' would be perfectly creamy white with a pink nose – perfect for harvesting!

Serves 4

200ml veal or chicken stock
60g butter
20 green asparagus spears,
    peeled (see Bruno's Tips)
1 tsp fresh rosemary (leave whole if fine,
    chopped if big)
1 tbsp nonpareille capers, rinsed
4 spring onions, sliced
1 tbsp roughly chopped flat-leaf parsley
salt and black pepper

Place the stock in a small pan, bring to the boil and bubble until reduced to half its volume.

Melt the butter in a large frying pan over a medium heat until foaming, then add the asparagus spears and rosemary, lining up the spears next to each other with all the tips facing the same way – this helps you control the cooking. Season with salt and pepper and cook for 3–4 minutes, using tongs to turn the asparagus and ensure even cooking, until tender when pierced with a sharp knife. Place the side of the pan with the asparagus tips off the heat source so they will cook slightly less. Add the stock and capers and bubble for about 30 seconds, scraping the bottom of the pan with a wooden spoon to deglaze it. Add the spring onions and parsley. Serve the asparagus with the pan juices drizzled over.

BRUNO'S TIPS

For this recipe I use green asparagus, but white will work equally well; they will just need a little extra cooking time.

· · ·

When peeling asparagus, place them flat on a chopping board and using a speed peeler, peel from the tip of the asparagus to the stem then rotate.

· · ·

You could also serve the asparagus sprinkled with grated Parmesan.

BEETROOT RAVIOLI 1997

I started making this dish about 15 years ago, perhaps even more, after seeing an Italian recipe in a magazine that I then adapted to my own liking. I think it has to be the longest surviving dish on my menu at the Bistrot. It also outsells any other and I would probably receive a threatening letter if I took it off the menu. We sell around 25 portions of this dish each day – that's around 70,000 pieces of ravioli a year!

Serves 6

500g Pasta Dough (see page 240)
fine semolina, to dust

Filling
500g beetroot, washed and dried
50ml balsamic vinegar
80g ricotta cheese
2 tbsp freshly grated Grana Padano
    or Parmesan cheese
salt and black pepper

Garnish
80g butter
2 tbsp panko breadcrumbs
8 sage leaves, finely sliced
2 handfuls of wild rocket
2 tbsp olive oil
½ tbsp lemon juice
2 tbsp freshly grated Grana Padano
    or Parmesan cheese
salt and black pepper

You will need to start preparing this recipe the day before you want to serve it.

Preheat the oven to 200°C/fan 180°C/ Gas 6. Wrap the beetroot in foil and bake in the oven for 2 hours. Remove and leave to cool then open the foil. Peel the beetroot, then cut into small dice. Transfer to a food processor and pulse in just three short bursts. Pour all the flesh out on to a clean tea towel or a double layer of muslin. Close it in a bundle and place in a colander set over a bowl. Cover the bundle with a plate and weigh it down with a 2kg weight. Place in the fridge overnight.

The next day, pour the beetroot juices into a small pan, add the balsamic vinegar and place over a low heat to reduce to a syrupy consistency. Watch it carefully as it will burn easily. When ready, pour into a small container.

Place the beetroot flesh in a mixing bowl with the ricotta, Grana Padano and a third of the beetroot juice reduction. Season with salt and pepper and mix well.

Roll out the pasta dough using a pasta machine. Start with the machine at its thickest setting and pass the dough through the rollers. Repeat several times, decreasing the setting and dusting the pasta with flour between each pass to prevent it from sticking to the rollers. Keep passing it until you have a very thin regular sheet, about 2mm thick. Place the pasta on a floured work surface.

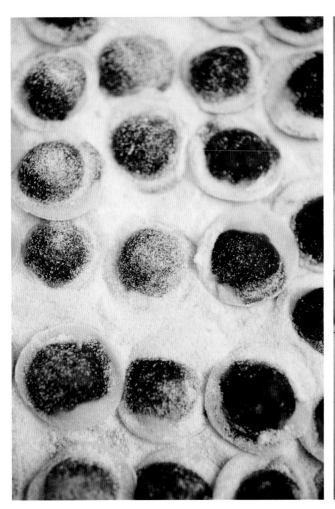

Transfer the filling to a piping bag and pipe balls of filling (about the size of a small cherry tomato) about 4cm apart over half the pasta sheet, then gently fold the other half back over it. Take a 3cm cookie cutter and using it upside down (i.e. the blunt not the cutting side) press down lightly over each mound to perfect the shape. Then with a 4.5cm cookie cutter, cut out each raviolo. Lift the excess dough away. Lightly dust a tray with semolina, then using a metal spatula, carefully transfer the ravioli to the tray.

For the garnish, heat 30g of the butter in a small frying pan and fry the breadcrumbs until golden and crisp.

Melt the remaining 50g of butter in a small pan with the sage. Heat until the butter starts to foam, then watch it carefully and as soon as it turns light brown, remove it from the heat and set aside.

Toss the rocket with the olive oil, lemon juice and seasoning. Place in the middle of each serving plate. Sprinkle the salad with the fried breadcrumbs and some grated Grana Padano.

Bring a deep pan of salted water to the boil. Meanwhile, gently reheat the sage butter. Cook the ravioli for 3 minutes, until they float, then drain carefully. Immediately toss the ravioli in the sage butter.

To serve, arrange the ravioli around the salad, drizzling it with a little of the butter. Finish the dish by drizzling over the remaining beetroot juice reduction. Serve immediately.

BRUNO'S TIPS

Don't bother making this yourself. Come to Bistrot Bruno Loubet instead.

GREEN LENTILS WITH ENDIVES & PEARS, ROQUEFORT DRESSING

Roquefort is the king of cheeses (for the French anyway!). Pair it with humble lentils, juicy pears and slightly bitter, crisp endive leaves and you have an interesting salad that will stand on its own as a starter but would also make a great accompaniment to roast pork.

Serves 4

250g puy or castelluccio lentils
3 thyme sprigs
1 small bay leaf
2 ripe Williams pears, thinly sliced
    (peeled if not ripe)
2 chicory heads (Belgian endives),
    leaves separated
½ red onion, chopped
20 tender celery leaves
50g Roquefort cheese
salt and black pepper

Dressing
50g Roquefort cheese
50ml walnut oil
80ml olive oil
30ml sherry vinegar
1 tbsp honey mustard
salt and pepper

Place the lentils, thyme and bay leaf in a pan with enough water to come 5cm above the lentils. Bring to the boil, then lower the heat to a simmer. Skim the surface, cover with a lid and leave to simmer for 20 minutes. The lentils should be soft but not broken.

Meanwhile, make the dressing. Put all the ingredients into a blender with some seasoning and blend until you have a smooth emulsion.

Drain the lentils, discarding the bay leaf and thyme. Place in a mixing bowl, pour over the dressing, mix well and leave to cool.

To serve, add the sliced pears, endives, onion and celery leaves to the lentils. Toss well, crumble over the Roquefort and serve.

BRUNO'S TIPS

I strongly advise mixing the dressing with the lentils while they are hot so that they will absorb its flavour. This is also a great tip for dressing a potato salad.

SMOKED CHICKEN
& CHEESE GOUGERE

When you entertain family and friends at home for a drink or before you sit down to a meal, it is always nice to have a few nibbles and the last thing you want to do is be slaving in the kitchen while your guests are enjoying good conversation and sipping the gems from your cellar! And if you want to keep your guests happy, then forget the barbecue-flavoured crisps, peanuts and pretzels and opt for just a couple of interesting nibbles. All you need is a small selection that will tickle the tastebuds with robust flavours, good seasoning, and of course, require no last-minute preparation! When serving these as a starter, I usually make a grated carrot salad with lemon and olive oil to accompany them.

Makes about 12

Choux
100ml milk, plus a little extra
80ml water
2 pinches of sugar
60g butter
125g plain flour
3 eggs
50g Grana Padano or Parmesan cheese,
*   finely grated*
50g Emmental cheese, finely grated
1 egg yolk, mixed with 6 tbsp milk
salt and black pepper

Filling
20g butter
20g flour
200ml milk
200g smoked chicken, finely diced
1 tsp chopped tarragon
1 tbsp crème fraîche
1 tbsp finely grated Grana Padano
*   or Parmesan cheese*
2 tbsp finely grated Emmental cheese
200ml strong chicken stock
freshly grated nutmeg, to taste
salt and pepper

Preheat the oven to 220°C/fan 200°C/ Gas 7. For the choux, put the milk, water, sugar and butter in a small saucepan and bring to the boil. As soon as it starts to boil, remove from the heat, then add the flour. Mix well with a wooden spoon, beating on one side of the pan until smooth. Return the pan to a medium heat for 1 minute, stirring continuously. Transfer the mix to a small mixing bowl, add the eggs one at a time, beating energetically after each one. The mixture should be smooth and shiny. Add three-quarters of each of the grated cheeses and mix in quickly.

Pour the mixture into a piping bag fitted with a plain 1cm nozzle. Line a baking sheet with greaseproof paper and pipe small walnut-sized balls over the paper, spacing them at least 3cm apart. Dip a fork in a little milk and mark the top of each ball with the back of a fork (this ensures more even cooking), then brush a little egg wash over each one. Sprinkle the tops with a little of the remaining cheese (reserve the remainder for serving).

Bake for 15–20 minutes, until the choux are crisp on the outside and lightly soft inside. Transfer to a cooling rack immediately. Leave to cool completely before filling.

For the filling, melt the butter in a small saucepan over a medium heat until foaming, then whisk in the flour. Cook for 30 seconds, then pour in the cold milk, whisking continuously to avoid lumps. Lower the heat to a simmer and cook for 5 more minutes, whisking continuously, then add the chicken, tarragon, crème fraîche and the cheeses. Adjust the seasoning with salt, pepper and nutmeg. Put the filling in a piping bag fitted with a small plain nozzle just large enough to let the chicken pass through. Push the nozzle into the underside of the choux buns and fill. Alternatively, cut the choux in half horizontally and fill using a teaspoon.

To serve, put the buns on a baking sheet, sprinkle with the reserved cheese and heat them in the oven for about 3 minutes.

WHOLEMEAL BREAD, LEMON & SPINACH DUMPLINGS IN TOMATO BROTH

Wanting to remain diplomatic (I know how Italians feel about their food!) I purposefully did not call this pasta 'passatelli' because this is my version of the dumpling/noodle speciality and a mix of different recipes. Travelling through Italy I tried different variations on the basic concept. In Tuscany a little spinach and grated lemon zest is added to the dough, in Le Marche they flavour them with nutmeg and in Romagna they will add a little flour. In my recipe I add fine semolina, which gives the dumplings a nice texture.

Serves 4

3 tbsp olive oil
2 handfuls of spinach
6 slices of good-quality wholemeal bread
1 tbsp fine semolina
2 pinches of grated nutmeg
2 eggs
1 tsp finely grated lemon zest
2 tbsp finely grated Parmesan cheese,
    plus extra to serve (optional)

Broth
4 tbsp olive oil
150g leeks, trimmed and thinly sliced
2 garlic cloves, chopped
½ tsp thyme leaves
1 x 400g can good-quality
    chopped tomatoes
1 litre chicken stock
salt and black pepper

For the broth, heat the olive oil over a medium heat, then add the leeks and season with salt and pepper. Stir well and sweat gently for about 8–10 minutes, to soften without colouring. Add the garlic, thyme, tomatoes and stock. Bring to the boil, skim the surface, then lower the heat, partly cover with a lid and simmer for 1 hour.

Meanwhile, prepare the pasta. Heat 2 tablespoons of the olive oil in a frying pan. Wilt the spinach for a minute. Drain and pat dry, then chop finely.

Place all the remaining ingredients for the pasta (except the spinach) in a food processor. Process until smooth.

When ready to serve, bring the broth to the boil, then lower to a simmer. Place the pasta mix in a colander and with the help of a plastic pastry scraper or spatula, push the pasta dough through the colander holes into the simmering broth. Work quickly as you want the pasta to cook uniformly. Simmer the pasta for 2 minutes then drain and rinse under cold water. Return the pasta to the frying pan and stir through the remaining tablespoon of olive oil, then tip the pasta back into the broth, along with the spinach.

Serve immediately with grated Parmesan, if wished.

BRUNO'S TIPS

My daughters love this with strong flavours so they always stir pesto into their broth.

• • •

Served with leftover roast chicken, this would make a fantastic main course dish.

STILTON FRITTERS
WITH PEAR & SOUR HONEY

This dish is one of my family's favourites to have in the evening served with extra salad. When you bite into them, the puffed, crisp fritters deliver a hot, light Stiltony mixture, which is delicious with the grilled pears and radish salad. It's actually a very simple starter to prepare and the mix could be made up the day before, leaving plenty of time to prepare your main course on the day.

Serves 4

4 tbsp, plus 1 tsp milk
4 tbsp, plus 1 tsp water
½ tsp caster sugar
75g plain flour
2 eggs, lightly beaten
200g Stilton, mashed with a fork
4 pinches of freshly grated nutmeg
2 pears, cored and cut lengthways
    into 6 wedges
4 tbsp olive oil, plus extra to serve
vegetable oil, to deep-fry
10 radishes, sliced
a handful of celery leaves or watercress
1 tbsp sherry vinegar
2 tbsp clear honey
salt and black pepper

Place the milk, water, sugar and a pinch of salt in a small saucepan and bring to the boil. Remove from the heat and add the flour, mixing well with a wooden spoon to break up any lumps. Return it to a low heat for 1 minute, mixing all the time, then remove and add the eggs a little at a time, continuing to mix until all the eggs are absorbed and the mixture is smooth and shiny. At this stage, add the cheese, nutmeg and some pepper. Mix well and set aside.

Heat a cast-iron griddle until hot. Place the pears on a plate. Toss in the olive oil and season with salt and pepper, then grill the pears, marking them on both sides – they will need about a minute on each side.

For a professional presentation you can shape the fritters into quenelles then place on a sheet of lightly oiled greaseproof paper, alternatively you can put the mixture into a piping bag fitted with a 15mm plain nozzle and pipe balls of the mixture on to the paper.

Heat enough vegetable oil for deep-frying in a deep-fat fryer or deep saucepan to 170°C (or check the oil is hot enough by dropping in a tiny amount of the fritter batter – it should brown quickly). Deep-fry the fritters in batches – this will take about 4 minutes per batch. Place on kitchen paper to drain.

To serve, arrange the fritters on serving plates with the pears, radishes and celery leaves or watercress. Mix the vinegar and honey then drizzle over the plates. Drizzle over some olive oil and finish with a crack of pepper.

BRUNO'S TIPS

Adding very small pieces of diced cooked ham or leftover roast chicken to the fritter mix makes them even better.

PETITS FARCIS DE PROVENCE
BLACK PUDDING & SCOTCH EGG
GRILLED OILY FISH
MARINATED LAMB SHOULDER
SHREDDED CHINESE CABBAGE,
CASHEW NUT & DUCK SALAD
ROLLED LAMB BREAST
POT ROAST PHEASANT
MAPLE CRISP DUCK BREAST
ROAST PARTRIDGE
ROASTED VENISON
WET ROAST PORK BELLY
BAKED BRIE
VEAL BLANQUETTE
SPICY CHICKEN LIVERS
CHICKEN MEATBALLS
GREY BREAM FILLET
TROUT FILLET
SAUTEED GURNARD

SALMON CONFIT
PORK RIBS
BRAISED BEEF CHEEKS
GUINEA FOWL
GRILLED MARINATED QUAIL
SUSTAINABLE BOUILLABAISSE
COTE DE BOEUF
WILD PIGEON
MY SPAGHETTI BORDELAISE
WILD RABBIT
TURKEY PAUPIETTE
TURKEY & BLUE CHEESE
MACKEREL WITH SALTED
& COMPRESSED WATERMELON
CALVES' LIVER
VEGETABLE COUSCOUS

MAIN COURSES

PETITS FARCIS DE PROVENCE

Many artists have been inspired by the light, smells and colours of Provence. Go to a local market in a Provençal village and somehow you can't help getting excited by the bounty of riches. It feels as if there is a natural energy around, a feel-good factor! This is a place you associate with holiday and friends, very much like its cooking. Stuffed vegetables are a great Provençal dish to cook for a big party because you can precook them and simply reheat them just before serving. Served directly from the cooking dish, these look great and of course, to complete the Provençal experience, make sure you have some rosé in the fridge.

Serves 6

6 mini aubergines
6 small squashes
6 red onions
6 vine-ripe tomatoes
4 tbsp olive oil
1 x 400g can good-quality
   chopped tomatoes
a handful of black olives
2 garlic cloves, chopped
12 sage leaves, chopped
1 tbsp rosemary leaves
1 tsp thyme leaves

Farce (stuffing)
200g semolina couscous
1 tbsp olive oil
about 100ml boiling water
2 tbsp basil leaves
2 tbsp flat-leaf parsley
100g soft goats' cheese
2 tbsp dried breadcrumbs
4 garlic cloves, finely chopped
50g Parmesan cheese
1 egg, lightly beaten
salt and black pepper

Preheat the oven to 195°C/fan 175°C/ Gas 5½.

Cut the tops off the vegetables and scoop out the centres with a small knife or spoon. Cut all the vegetable insides finely and place in a small pan with 2 tablespoons of the olive oil. Cook them over a low heat until soft, then remove from the heat and set aside.

For the *farce*, place the couscous in a bowl, season with salt and add the olive oil. Pour over the boiling water, mix well, then press the top with the back of the spoon to compress the couscous. Cover with cling film and leave to absorb the water for about 5 minutes.

Place the cooked vegetable trimmings in a food processor with the herbs, goats' cheese and breadcrumbs. Process until well chopped, then place in a bowl with the couscous, Parmesan and egg. Mix well with a spoon and check the seasoning.

You need to start to cook the vegetables before they go in the oven.

Heat the remaining 2 tablespoons of olive oil in a roasting tin placed over a medium heat. Add the hollowed-out aubergines, squash and onions and start to colour them all over – this should take about 4 minutes. Once lightly coloured, turn the heat off, lift the vegetables out of the tin and add the tomatoes, olives, garlic and herbs. Stir to mix.

Fill the vegetables with the *farce*, then replace them in the roasting tin on top of the tomato mixture. Place the tin in the oven for 30 minutes, until the vegetables are soft and the stuffing is piping hot.

BRUNO'S TIPS

If you like you can add 150g of minced lamb to the *farce* but you will need to reduce the quantities of couscous and goats' cheese to 50g. Add the uncooked lamb when you add the Parmesan and egg.

BLACK PUDDING & SCOTCH EGG SALAD WITH HORSERADISH DRESSING

I've never understood why haggis rarely makes it into the ingredients list for Scotch eggs but this recipe will change all that. This dish is testament to how a few well-chosen ingredients can be combined to look and taste so good; there is a sophisticated 'pub' feel to it and I think it makes a perfect Sunday lunch for family and friends.

Serves 6

1 x 300g Scottish haggis
3 of your favourite sausages,
    skinned and broken up
10 eggs
1 tbsp chopped sage
100g flour
200g dried breadcrumbs
500g black pudding, cut into 6 slices
40g butter
vegetable oil, for deep-frying the eggs

Salad
180g curly endive
2 handfuls of mâche (lamb's lettuce)
1 red onion, sliced
3 tbsp sliced gherkins
a small handful of flat-leaf
    parsley leaves

Dressing
7 tbsp walnut oil
2 tbsp good-quality red wine vinegar
2 tbsp creamed horseradish
salt and black pepper

First make the Scotch eggs. Open the haggis and place the filling in a bowl with the sausage meat. Add two eggs and the chopped sage. Wearing rubber gloves mix well with your hands.

Place six eggs in boiling salted water and cook for 4 minutes. Refresh in cold water, leave to cool, then peel off the shells.

Divide the haggis mixture into six and shape into balls. Place one ball on a plate and flatten to a 10cm circle. Place a boiled egg in the middle then encase the egg in the haggis. Finish by rolling the Scotch egg between wet hands to give it a regular shape. Repeat with the other boiled eggs. Transfer to a plate and place in the fridge to chill.

Mix all the ingredients for the dressing.

Lightly beat the two remaining eggs and place in a small, shallow dish. Place the flour in another shallow dish and the breadcrumbs in a third. Roll each Scotch egg in the flour, then in the egg wash, then in the breadcrumbs.

Heat enough oil for deep-frying in a large, deep pan or deep-fat fryer. When the oil is hot enough (170°C) fry the eggs until golden brown (you can do this in two batches if necessary). Transfer to kitchen paper to drain.

To serve, mix the salad ingredients with the dressing in a bowl then divide among six plates. Pan-fry the black pudding slices in the butter for about 3 minutes on each side. Place the black pudding slices on the salad. Cut each Scotch egg in half and arrange on the salad. Serve immediately.

GRILLED OILY FISH
WITH A GREEN MEXICAN SAUCE

During a sojourn in Los Angeles I tried as much Mexican food as I could, some good and some not so good. One dish particularly attracted my attention for its simplicity and amazing flavours. It was grilled fish with a green sauce. The sauce was refreshing with different layers of clean flavours. Back in Australia I started to serve my version of it with 'barbies' and everyone loved it too. Friends even suggested that I bottle it and it would become the next Tabasco success story!

Serves 6

6 portions of oily fish (such as mackerel,
*   salmon or sardines), with skin*
olive oil, for grilling
salt and black pepper

Sauce
⅓ cucumber
½ jalapeño chilli, finely chopped
1 garlic clove, finely chopped
a small handful of mint leaves
a large handful of coriander,
*   finely chopped*
1 tbsp fresh oregano leaves
4 spring onions, finely chopped
½ tsp muscovado sugar
juice of 1 lime
50ml olive oil
⅓ tsp ground toasted cumin seeds
salt

Prepare all the ingredients for the sauce while the barbecue is heating – you need to make the sauce while the fish is cooking so that it's as fresh as possible.

To grill the fish, prepare the barbecue or heat the griddle until hot. Brush the fish with olive oil, season with salt and pepper then grill on the barbecue or on the griddle on each side, until cooked (the cooking time will depend on the type and size of the fish you choose).

Meanwhile, place all the sauce ingredients in a blender with two ice cubes and blitz until smooth. Transfer to a serving bowl and serve alongside the grilled fish.

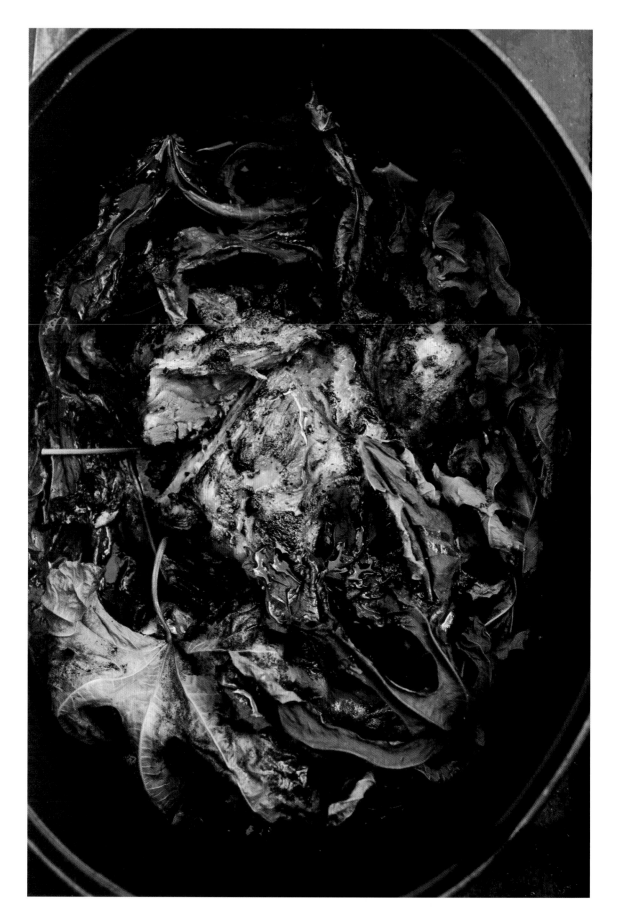

MARINATED LAMB SHOULDER POT ROASTED WITH FIG LEAVES

A few months after the opening of the Bistrot I received a phone call from a man called Jody Scheckter asking me to participate in the British barbecue championship organised on his fabulous Laverstoke Park Farm. I met Jody and quickly realised he was an extremely competitive man (this explains his past success in Formula One racing). At Laverstoke, Jody has taken on board a mammoth project, creating a 2,500-acre organic, biodynamic farm in Hampshire. His beliefs and focus have paid off and the farm is now producing not one or two, but a multitude of award-winning delicacies. On the day of the barbecue final, I arrived late with only a few ingredients I'd thrown together in a hurry. It was the most glorious English summer day so I decided to go around the farm foraging. I came across a lovely fig tree that reminded me of how my mother used to cook chestnuts with fig leaves to add flavour. I picked some leaves and used them to wrap the fantastic lamb I had been given on arrival at the farm. The lamb was simply marinated, seared on the 'barbie', then wrapped in the leaves and finished slowly. I served it with a simple shaved raw vegetable salad and won the competition! I have since enjoyed Laverstoke Farm's fantastic produce and Jody's friendship.

Serves 6

1.5kg boned lamb shoulder
100g natural yoghurt
juice of ½ lemon
2 garlic cloves, chopped
1 tsp chopped marjoram
1 tsp crushed green peppercorns
olive oil, for cooking on the barbecue
6 fig leaves, washed
salt and black pepper

Salad
10 baby carrots, finely sliced
10 baby fennel heads, finely sliced
12 breakfast radishes, finely sliced
1 red onion, finely sliced
6 baby courgettes, finely sliced
12 cherry tomatoes
100g peas, or frozen petit
   pois, defrosted
12 mint leaves
2 tbsp chopped flat-leaf
   parsley, shredded
1 tbsp basil leaves

Dressing
4 tbsp olive oil
juice of ½ lemon
juice of ½ orange
1 tsp honey mustard
salt and black pepper

If the lamb has a layer of fat, use a sharp knife to shave it off, bit by bit, until you reach the flesh.

Put the yoghurt in a bowl with the lemon juice, garlic, marjoram, peppercorns and seasoning. Mix well with a small whisk or a fork then roll the shoulder in this mix, rubbing it all over with your fingers.

Place the lamb and all its marinade in a plastic bag, using a spatula to make sure you scoop up all the marinade. Tie a knot in the bag to seal. Massage the lamb well then place in the fridge and leave to marinate (see Bruno's Tips).

To allow the marinade and the heat to get into the meat before it burns, the lamb has to start cooking at a fairly low temperature.

Light the barbecue to low, then place the meat on the griddle, close the lid or place a pot over the meat if you don't have a lid. After 20 minutes, the meat will be starting to brown. Brush the lamb gently with a little olive oil, then remove from the barbecue and bring the temperature up.

Replace the lamb and cook the shoulder for about 3–4 minutes on each side to deepen the colour, then remove and wrap it in the fig leaves.

Next wrap it in a sheet of foil or place it inside a cocotte. Leave the foil or the cocotte slightly open. Reduce the heat of the barbecue to its minimum and return the foil parcel or the cocotte to the heat. The meat will finish cooking very slowly – it will need another 20 minutes – absorbing the flavour of the fig leaves.

Remove from the heat and leave the lamb to rest for at least 10 minutes. Meanwhile, prepare the salad. Place all the salad ingredients in a large bowl.

Ten minutes before serving, mix the ingredients for the dressing, check the seasoning then pour over the salad and mix gently.

Place the lamb on a carving board, pour its juices over the salad and carve the meat at the table.

BRUNO'S TIPS

In spring or summer you are most likely to be buying young lamb. The meat will be tender so you will only need to marinate it for 45 minutes. In autumn and winter, the meat will be taken from a large shoulder from an older animal and it will need marinating for longer – 6–8 hours to tenderise it.

SHREDDED CHINESE CABBAGE, CASHEW NUT & DUCK SALAD

Confit used to be a form of preserving when refrigeration wasn't common; however, it's now a cooking technique used mostly for the resulting flavours and textures. In my family we used to confit meats regularly: often duck, of course, but also pork and even chicken. The irony of this cooking method is that you will only get a good result if you don't use prime cuts – working muscles, such as duck and chicken legs, lamb shanks and pork knuckles or shoulder, are preferable to lean cuts as the lack of fat means that the latter will dry out. This is also a thrifty means of cooking – the fat used for the confit can be passed through a fine sieve and stored in the fridge for future use.

I love the crunchy texture of the Chinese cabbage in this salad, which makes it fresh and light at the same time. If you have the confit ready-made and stored in the fridge, this dish is perfect to serve up for unexpected guests as it is very quick to put together.

Serves 6

Duck confit
6 duck legs
2 tbsp sea salt
½ tsp pepper
1 garlic clove, chopped
½ tsp thyme leaves
1 tbsp brandy
500ml duck or goose fat
1 glass of white wine
80g cashew nuts, toasted

You also need a cooking thermometer
(ingredients continued overleaf)

You will need to prepare the duck confit in advance. Place the legs skin-side down in a shallow dish. Sprinkle evenly with the salt, pepper, garlic and thyme, then drizzle over the brandy. Cover with cling film and store in the fridge overnight (or for at least 12 hours).

The next day, rinse the duck under cold water, then pat dry. Place in a large pan with the duck fat and white wine. Melt the duck fat until it reaches a temperature of 90°C. Adjust the heat to maintain this temperature, then cover with foil and leave to cook for 2½ hours.

Preheat the oven to 240°C/fan 220°C/ Gas 9. Check to see whether the duck is cooked by inserting a small fine knife blade into a leg; it should come out without any resistance.

Remove from the heat and leave the legs to rest in the fat for 30 minutes,

Vegetables

1 Chinese cabbage, finely shredded
6 spring onions, finely sliced
2 garlic cloves, finely sliced
25g fresh root ginger, cut into
    very fine strips
1 tsp finely chopped green chilli
a handful of fresh coriander leaves

Dressing

1 tbsp sesame oil
3 tbsp olive oil
2 tbsp dark soy sauce
4 tbsp creamed horseradish
2 tbsp good-quality red wine vinegar
1 tbsp honey mustard

then lift out and place in a roasting tin, skin-side up. Add a small wineglass of water and cook in the oven for about 6 minutes or until the skin crisps. At this stage, remove from the oven and set aside to rest.

Put all the ingredients for the dressing in a small saucepan and heat gently. Remove the flesh and skin from the duck legs and break it up (discard the bones), then place in a mixing bowl.

Add the vegetables, pour over the warm dressing, then add the cashew nuts. Mix well and divide among six plates. Serve immediately.

BRUNO'S TIPS

To store the duck fat after cooking the legs, strain it through a fine sieve, transfer to an airtight container and place in the fridge. After becoming solid in the fridge, the fat will have a layer of jellified stock at the bottom. Separate it from the fat and use as flavouring in the dressing of this dish or in a soup or pasta sauce. The fat can be kept in the fridge for up to one month.

• • •

Another simple way to crisp the confit skin is to put it in a frying pan with a bit of the fat over a low heat, until coloured and crisp.

ROLLED LAMB BREAST,
CONFIT WITH FENNEL SEEDS,
ORANGE & SUMAC

Rack, leg, shoulder and sometimes lamb shank are the cuts you will commonly find in cookbooks but breast is rarely used. I've decided to buck the trend. I think we should learn to cook with products that are not so common on our supermarket shelves. After all, we should remember that as consumers, we are the ones creating the demand for products. Like many chefs, I feel I have a duty to respect the food chain to preserve it for future generations and making the most of the whole animal is part of that. Our modern world is all about convenience: fine cuts are easier to butcher but they command higher prices. Because they're so tender, there's less time and effort involved in the cooking, which is a fair argument but we pay the price in the long run. And it does not actually mean they are better – often they are not as tasty. Lamb breast is now available in shops. Create and support the demand by trying new cuts. You may find new favourites in the process.

Serves 4

700g lamb breast, bone removed,
    rolled and tied (ask your butcher to
    do this for you)
1 tbsp sumac
3 tbsp mango chutney
1 tsp fennel seeds, toasted and crushed
1 tsp grated orange zest
1 aubergine, sliced crossways
1 large onion, finely sliced
3 garlic cloves, crushed
8 sprigs of fresh thyme
salt and black pepper

Preheat the oven to 195°C/fan 175°C/ Gas 5½.

Cut the string and open the breast of lamb, season lightly on both sides with the sumac, salt and pepper. Spread the mango chutney on one side, sprinkle over the fennel seeds and orange zest, then roll the breast up again tightly. Tie it with string to hold it firmly then roll in a 40cm piece of foil.

Place the roll in an ovenproof dish and pour 300ml of water into the bottom of the dish. Place in the oven and cook for 3 hours, turning it every 30 minutes, so that it cooks evenly.

Meanwhile, salt the aubergine, place in a colander and leave to rest for 20 minutes. Rinse with cold water, then heat a cast-iron griddle. Grill the

aubergine slices on both sides, until marked with char lines and tender. Place the aubergine under the lamb after 2½ hours of cooking, with the onion, garlic and thyme sprigs, and leave to cook for the remainder of the cooking time.

To serve, open the foil over the dish to preserve the juices. Remove the foil and place the lamb over the aubergine again. Cut off the strings and discard.

Slice the lamb breast and serve with the aubergines and onions, spooning the juices over.

POT ROAST PHEASANT
WITH CELERY SALT & POMEGRANATE MOLASSES, BREAD & BACON PUDDING

Personally I've never been a fan of hanging game birds for a long period as the French do. The idea behind the process is to tenderise the flesh and improve its flavour but to me it just gives the meat too strong a flavour and a smell that I don't like. I'm a bit of a let-down as a Frenchman! In place of the hanging I use a marinade. In this recipe, the acidity from the yoghurt in the sweet and sour marinade will help to tenderise the meat and the sweetness from the sugar content will colour and glaze the surface. The steam in the pot will also keep the moisture in the meat. Who said pheasant was boring?

Serves 4

2 oven-ready pheasants
2 large potatoes
50ml white wine
1 bay leaf
4 sprigs of fresh thyme
100ml veal or dark chicken stock

Marinade

4 tbsp natural yoghurt
4 tbsp pomegranate molasses
2 tbsp celery salt
2 garlic cloves, chopped
freshly ground black pepper
2 tbsp brandy

Pudding

30g butter, plus extra for greasing
200g smoked streaky bacon, cut into
    small dice or strips
200g brown onions, finely sliced
2 garlic cloves, finely chopped
50ml sherry
60ml cream
4 slices of white bread, crusts removed
2 large sage leaves
1 egg

You will need to start marinating the pheasants the day before you want to serve the dish. Put all the ingredients for the marinade into a bowl and mix well. Place the pheasants in a dish and brush the marinade all over them, using a pastry brush. Wrap the birds in cling film and place in the fridge overnight.

The next day, preheat the oven to 160°C/fan 140°C/Gas 3.

Start by making the pudding. Butter four ramekins (7cm in diameter; see

Bruno's Tips.) Melt the butter in a frying pan over a low heat. Add the bacon, onions and garlic, cover with a lid and cook gently, stirring two or three times, to avoid any colouration but to melt some of the fat and soften the onions – this will take about 15 minutes.

Remove from the heat, then pour into a blender, add the sherry, cream, bread, sage and finally the egg. Blend until smooth. Pass the mixture through a fine sieve, pushing it down with the back of a small ladle or spoon.

Divide the pudding mixture between the buttered ramekins. Place the ramekins in an ovenproof dish lined with non-stick baking paper and pour in enough hot water to come halfway up the sides of the ramekins. Cover the dish with foil and make two little holes in the top. Place in the oven for 20 minutes.

When cooked, take the dish out of the oven and set aside with the foil still on. Increase the oven to 200°C/fan 180°C/Gas 6.

Peel the potatoes and cut each into two equal pieces, then cut a piece off the curved sides to flatten them slightly. Put the potatoes into a large casserole, and place the pheasants on top. Pour in the white wine, add the bay leaf and thyme, then cover with a lid and place in the oven for about 30 minutes.

Open the pheasant pot, add the stock and leave to cook for another 10 minutes. Meanwhile, reheat the puddings by putting the roasting tin directly on to the stove top and warming them in their water bath over a low heat.

To serve, remove the pheasants from the pot. Detach the legs from the bodies, cut off the drumsticks and discard. Cut along the breast bones to detach the breasts.

Divide the potatoes among the serving plates, then sit one breast and one thigh on top. Unmould the puddings and place one on each plate, then spoon the juices over. Serve immediately.

MAPLE CRISP DUCK BREAST
WITH WALNUT PESTO

In my native south west, duck is part of our culture. As a child, one of my jobs when I came home from school in the afternoon was to feed the chickens, pigeons, rabbits and ducks. In the winter, my brother and I were given the task of force-feeding the ducks to fatten them. My mother used to produce an amazing selection of riches from the ducks: rillettes, confits, stuffed necks, *grattons* (pieces of duck skin cooked in duck fat until crispy, then seasoned with garlic, mace and brandy) and foie gras. Even the bones were used to make a tasty bouillon, which any mother would freeze until she needed it for making *garbure* (a thick cabbage and root vegetable soup from Gascony). The breasts or *magrets* were usually cooked very rare on embers made of vine cuttings and seasoned with crushed green peppercorns. I never liked my meat very rare; I was definitely the black sheep of the family!

In this recipe, I caramelise the duck skin with maple syrup and green peppercorns, which is reminiscent of the Asian style of cooking, but I keep the meat very pink – South West France-style. Perfect yin and yang.

Serves 4

4 duck breasts
5 tbsp maple syrup
3 tbsp good-quality red wine vinegar
1 tbsp crushed green peppercorns
salt and black pepper
Braised Celery (see page 171),
    to serve (optional)

Pesto
100g walnuts
1 large sage leaf
100ml olive oil
25ml white wine
1 slice of wholemeal bread,
    crust removed
50g Grana Padano or Parmesan
    cheese, grated
black pepper

Start by making the pesto. Place the walnuts, sage, olive oil and white wine in a food processor. Process until very fine, then add the bread. Give the mixture a blitz, then add the Grana Padano and give it another blitz – it should be a textured rather than smooth pesto. Season with pepper. Pour into a small bowl and set aside.

Season the duck breasts and place them skin-side down in a frying pan (see Bruno's Tips). Place over a medium heat and after a few minutes, the fat will start to render and help to cook the duck. Leave the breasts until the skin is golden brown, about 8 minutes. By that time the flesh should be starting to cook, too.

Flip the breasts over and reduce the heat to low. You want to cook the breasts gently so that the flesh doesn't dry out. After two minutes remove the breasts to a plate. Pour the fat though a fine sieve set over a bowl, then transfer to an airtight container and refrigerate (see Bruno's Tips).

Pour the maple syrup, vinegar and green peppercorns into the pan and bubble vigorously to reduce to a glaze, then put the duck breasts back in the pan, skin-side down. Swirl the pan to move the glaze around and coat the duck. After two minutes, turn the duck over and leave for a minute on this side, then remove the breasts from the pan and leave to rest for a few minutes.

To serve, cut the duck into thick slices. Place on plates, spoon over the glaze and place a spoonful of walnut pesto on the side. Serve with Braised Celery or try it with the Crushed Root Vegetables with Duck Fat (see page 165).

BRUNO'S TIPS

Duck breasts in the UK are generally not as large as in France. In France the layer of fat under the skin is thick and you need to shave it off so that there is just 2mm left. In the UK, the duck breasts are thinner and have less fat so there is no need to score or trim them before cooking. When buying duck breasts, buy ones that are as thick as possible as the thinner breasts don't have enough fat and will therefore be tougher. Store the rendered duck fat in an airtight container (see page 86) and use it for making roast potatoes or vegetables, or even add a spoonful to a soup to enrich it – very welcome in winter.

ROAST PARTRIDGE
ON GINGER & SOY BRUSSELS SPROUTS

Brussels sprouts carry a stigma! Many people remember school dinners served with overcooked sprouts, which were an unattractive brown colour and smelt like wet dogs. They do not need to be like that. In this recipe, I give sprouts an Asian twist, which is great with the light, gamey flavour of the partridge.

Serves 6

100g butter
6 oven-ready partridges
600g Brussels sprouts, trimmed
*   and finely sliced*
200g small turnips, peeled and
*   finely sliced*
100g shallots, sliced
2 garlic cloves, sliced
4 sprigs of fresh thyme
4 tbsp cider vinegar
2 tbsp elderflower cordial
400ml veal or dark chicken stock
30g butter
50ml olive oil
30g fresh root ginger, peeled
*   and chopped*
50ml soy sauce
salt and black pepper

Preheat the oven to 200°C/fan 180°C/Gas 6.

Heat the butter in a large casserole until foaming. Add the partridges and brown lightly on each side, then transfer to a roasting tin and place in the oven for about 8 minutes, turning them from one side to the other then on to their backs. Remove from the oven and leave to rest breast-side down in the tin.

Steam the Brussels sprouts and turnip for about a minute, just to soften them slightly, or plunge them into boiling salted water for 30 seconds, then drain.

Lift the partridges out of the roasting tin and place on a warm dish covered with foil. Discard some of the fat from the tin, leaving just a little in which to colour the shallots, garlic and thyme. Place the tin over a medium heat, and add the shallots, garlic and thyme.

When coloured, pour in the vinegar and cordial, increase the heat and bring to a vigorous boil, then add the stock, scraping the bottom of the tin with a wooden spoon to deglaze the pan and extract all the partridge

residue. Pour the liquid into a smaller saucepan then add an ice cube (see Bruno's Tips), bring to the boil, skim the surface, and boil until reduced to a nice sauce consistency. You should get about 150ml of sauce.

Pass the sauce through a fine sieve, then return to the pan and bring back to the boil. Stir in the butter. Taste and adjust the seasoning if necessary.

Meanwhile, heat the olive oil in a wok over a high heat and add the Brussels sprouts, turnips and the ginger. Stir well for 30 seconds, then add the soy sauce, lower the heat to medium and cook for 3 minutes.

You can serve the partridges on the bone with the Brussels sprouts next to it and the juice all over, or bone them and place them on top of the sprouts with the sauce over and around them.

BRUNO'S TIPS

Placing ice cubes in a sauce will help you to 'clean' it as the ice cubes make the fat rise so that it is easier to skim it off.

ROASTED VENISON
WITH CRUSHED CELERIAC & COFFEE-INFUSED SAUCE

I keep telling my chef friends around the world that the UK is so privileged with its game. During the game season, a huge variety and quantity is available in butcher's shops and supermarkets, which is fantastic and a chef's dream! Venison is quite expensive so it is a treat, but what a lovely treat. It's free of fat and has a high iron content, which makes this deep, red meat healthy and delicious. However, venison will dry out quickly if overcooked, so rare and well rested is the way to go. If you like your meat cooked more than medium-rare, then don't waste your money on roasted venison loin; braised shank or shoulder will be better for you as these can be cooked until well done but still tender.

Serves 4

600g celeriac, peeled and diced
100g butter
200ml milk
½ tsp celery salt
700g venison loin
2 tbsp vegetable oil
salt and black pepper

Sauce
2 tbsp vegetable oil
venison trimmings (optional)
120g shallots, finely sliced
1 garlic clove, crushed
2 sprigs of fresh thyme
½ bay leaf
150ml red wine
1 tbsp quince jelly
120ml veal or beef stock
6 coffee beans, crushed
25g butter

Start by making the sauce. If you manage to get some venison trimmings (see Bruno's Tips), colour them in the oil in a frying pan for a few minutes. Add the shallots, garlic, thyme and bay leaf and cook over a medium heat until golden brown. Pour in the wine and bring to a vigorous boil, scraping the base of the pan with a wooden spoon to deglaze it. Boil for a minute, then add the quince jelly and the stock. Bring back to the boil, then lower the heat to a slow simmer. Skim the surface and leave to simmer for about 40 minutes.

Meanwhile, cook the celeriac. Preheat the oven to 195°C/fan 175°C/Gas 5½. Place the celeriac in an ovenproof dish with the butter and the milk. Season with the celery salt and some pepper and mix well. Cover the dish with a double layer of foil, sealing it tightly all around. Place in the oven for 20 minutes, then remove and set aside to rest.

When the sauce is shiny and has a good consistency, pass it through a fine sieve but do not press down on the solids. Pour half a glass of hot water over the shallots to make sure you get all the sauce. Return the sauce to the pan and bring back to the boil to reduce and achieve the same consistency. Add the crushed coffee beans to the sauce, then remove from the heat and set aside for the sauce to infuse.

Season the venison with salt and pepper. In a frying pan, heat the vegetable oil over a high heat and sear the venison all over to seal. Lower the

heat to medium and cook for a couple of minutes, without moving the meat, then remove from the heat, cover the pan with a lid and leave the venison to rest for 10 minutes.

Crush the cooked celeriac, then place in a small saucepan. Add any fat and juices from the meat.

Pass the sauce through a fine sieve set over a clean small saucepan. Add the butter and swirl the pan for the butter to dissolve completely.

To serve, slice the meat and serve with some crushed celeriac, then pour the sauce over.

BRUNO'S TIPS

In large supermarkets venison is usually sold already trimmed. If you buy venison from a butcher and it's already been trimmed, ask for some of the trimmings (about 250g) for your sauce. Coloured and stewed in the sauce, they will give it more depth of flavour.

• • •

The recipe also works well with hare or venison saddle in place of the loin.

• • •

Farmed venison is quite common these days and is perfectly good. If you like a stronger, more complex flavour then I suggest you marinate the meat for at least 24 hours prior to cooking as this brings out the gaminess. For the quantity of meat required for this recipe you will need: 4 crushed juniper berries, 2 pinches of ground cinnamon, 2 pinches of ground ginger, 1 tbsp gin, 5 tbsp red wine. Place all the ingredients in a small plastic food bag with all the meat and close tightly. Place in the fridge for 24 hours, moving the bag from time to time.

SOUR & SPICY
WET ROAST PORK BELLY
WITH PICKLED CABBAGE

Pork belly has been a very popular item on menus in the last few years but sadly I don't think people are cooking it at home very much. What a shame that is, as it is such a tasty cut of meat. It's important to choose a piece with a good ratio of meat to fat – in percentage terms about 70:30. The Chinese-inspired pickled cabbage is so easy to do and adds a fantastic finishing touch to the dish.

Serves 6

1.5kg pork belly
200ml white wine
3 tbsp sweet soy sauce
2 star anise
30g fresh root ginger, peeled and
    cut into very fine strips
2 tbsp Dijon mustard
1 orange, cut into quarters
1 lemon, cut into quarters
80ml vegetable oil
salt and black pepper

Pickled cabbage
750g Chinese cabbage, cut into 2cm dice,
    washed and patted dry
3 tbsp sea salt
2 tbsp brown sugar
60ml peanut oil
1 onion, chopped
2 red chillies, chopped
4 garlic cloves, chopped
30g fresh root ginger, chopped
1 tbsp Szechuan pepper
1 tsp English mustard
100ml brown rice vinegar
coriander leaves, to garnish

Start by making the pickled cabbage. Place the cabbage in a bowl. Sprinkle with the salt and sugar and mix well with your hands, squeezing the cabbage for two minutes (this bruises it and helps get the salt into it), then leave at room temperature for 2 hours, repeating the squeezing every 30 minutes.

Preheat the oven to 240°C/fan 220°C/Gas 9. In a wok, heat the peanut oil, then add the onions, chilli, garlic, ginger, Szechuan pepper and mustard. Stir-fry over a high heat for 10 seconds then lower the heat to medium and cook for 2–3 minutes to soften the ingredients. Meanwhile drain the cabbage and squeeze out any excess liquid.

Add the cabbage to the wok, stir and remove from the heat. Add the brown rice vinegar. Pour all the ingredients into a glass or china dish and cover with cling film.

For the pork, place the white wine, soy sauce, star anise, ginger, mustard, orange and lemon quarters in a pan and bring to a simmer, then cook for 2 minutes.

Place the belly in a roasting tin. Pour the mixture over then rub it all over the flesh but not the skin. Season with salt and pepper then pour the vegetable oil all over the meat. Arrange the fruit quarters under the belly and place it skin-side up.

Cook for about 20 minutes, keeping an eye on the level of the liquid to make sure it does not evaporate too much – there should always be a minimum of 2mm in the bottom. If needed, add a bit of water, then lower the oven setting to 170°C/fan 150°C/Gas 3½ and leave to cook for another 30 minutes.

Remove the meat from the oven and leave to rest for at least 10 minutes, then cut into six pieces.

Place a piece of belly on each plate with a mound of pickled cabbage on the side. Finish with some fresh coriander.

BAKED BRIE WITH POTATOES & HAM, FLAMBEED WITH GIN

Everyone is human, and sometimes (and I really mean only once in a while) you should let your guard down and enjoy a yummy, creamy comforting dish. In this recipe, the warm Brie, oozing between the layers of velvety potatoes, the saltiness of the ham and the dry alcoholic 'woof' of the gin could easily make this decadent dish your guilty pleasure – it's certainly one of mine.

Brie cheese is unfortunately one of those products whose quality has declined. Demand increased so supply had to increase with it, and this led to a rise of mass-market factory-produced cheese that bears little resemblance to Brie that is prepared in the correct way, using artisanal methods. The best ones to buy are Brie de Meaux and Brie de Melun, both of which hold the AOC. Brie fermier, Brie de Nangis and Brie de Coulommiers are also of a good standard. If an inferior quality Brie is used in this recipe, it will result in a plastery potato gratin so please do seek out a good one.

Serves 4

700g Desiree potatoes
500g Brie de Meaux
8 thin slices of Bayonne ham
gin, to taste (depending on how
    you feel!)
4 tbsp walnut oil
salt and black pepper

You will also need 4 metal rings (12cm x 3cm); see Bruno's Tips

Preheat the oven to 195°C/fan 175°C/Gas 5½.

Place the potatoes in a large pan. Cover with water and a bit of salt. Bring to the boil and boil until a thin knife blade goes into the potatoes easily, about 15 minutes. Drain, peel, then slice the potatoes 5–7mm thick. Slice the Brie roughly the same thickness.

Place each metal ring onto a large square of greaseproof paper and fold the excess paper around the bottom of the ring. Line the bottom of the rings with a layer of potatoes and seasoning, then a layer of ham, then Brie. Sprinkle with gin and walnut oil, then repeat the layers until you reach the top of the rings, finishing with the Brie and a sprinkling of gin and oil.

Place the rings on a baking tray and bake for 10–12 minutes, until the Brie is golden and bubbling, then slide each one onto a serving plate, add a last splash of gin over each one and lift off the rings.

Serve with a big bowl of crisp salad and a light bread, such as baguette.

BRUNO'S TIPS

For this dish I like to use metal rings for presentation but a gratin dish would work too. I also like to present it in a cheese box, which makes it more original.

MY GRANDMOTHER'S
VEAL BLANQUETTE

If I had to choose one dish to associate with my grandmother it would definitely have to be *blanquette de veau* – a French classic in which veal is stewed in a clear bouillon, which is then enriched with cream to make a white sauce. What made her recipe so unique was the unusual amount of celery and the large handful of finely chopped chervil she added at the very end with the lemon juice. The meat was chosen from the belly, shoulder and shank, cooked at an extremely low simmer, then rested in the bouillon until the next day when the sauce was finished with a roux, cream and egg yolk. This was a dish filled with love and care. For me it transcends home cooking like no other.

Serves 6

1.2kg diced veal from the shoulder,
    belly or shank
salt

Garnish
200g carrots, sliced
200g onions, cut into quarters
200g leeks (green part only),
    cut into chunks
400g celery (leaves and stalks),
    cut into chunks
3 garlic cloves, crushed
2 cloves
1 small bay leaf
3 sprigs of fresh thyme
200ml white wine
6 peppercorns, crushed

Sauce
25g butter
25g flour
150ml cream
250g button mushrooms, sliced
juice of ½ lemon
150g green beans, trimmed, and blanched
    in boiling water for 1 minute
5 tbsp roughly chopped chervil
celery salt

First, wash the meat with cold water and place in a large pan. Cover with cold water, add three pinches of salt and bring to the boil. When the liquid just starts to boil, lower the heat and skim the surface.

Add all the garnish ingredients, mix well with a large spoon then bring the liquid back to a gentle simmer and cook for 40 minutes, until the veal is cooked through. Remove from the heat and pass the mixture through a colander set over a large pan. Return the bouillon to the heat and reduce to 600ml. Cover the meat and vegetables with cling film to stop them drying out (see Bruno's Tips).

For the sauce, melt the butter in a medium stainless steel or ceramic pan (not copper or aluminum) until foaming. Add the flour, mix well with a whisk for 1 minute, then pour the bouillon over it in a fine stream, whisking continuously to avoid lumps forming. Bring to the boil, then lower the heat to a simmer, then add the cream and mushrooms. Leave to cook for 15 minutes, then add the meat and vegetables to reheat them in the sauce. Just before serving add the lemon juice, green beans and the chopped chervil and season with celery salt.

BRUNO'S TIPS

Covering the cooked meat and vegetables in cling film stops them from drying out – as the heat evaporates and condenses, the cling film traps all the condensation so all the moisture is locked in.

• • •

Prep it all the day before but don't strain the meat; leave it to cool in its bouillon, then refrigerate. Reheat the veal in the bouillon and finish the sauce with the butter and flour on the day.

RAMMA'S
SPICY CHICKEN LIVERS

Ramma is a very good friend of ours from Indian Fiji. She lives in Brisbane and is married to one of my best friends, Dermy, an energetic Irish man with a larger-than-life personality. Ramma's cooking is starting to gain quite a following and their circle of friends is growing endlessly due to their generosity. Dermy is so proud of his wife's talent that he keeps inviting people to come and enjoy her family's culinary heritage. One of my great favourites is her chicken livers, which she always cooks when I am around. She serves them as a nibble with a delicious fried yoghurt bread but she won't give me the recipe for the bread as it's a family secret. I love them so much that I often serve them at home as a main course, replacing her yoghurt bread with naan bread and some yoghurt on the side. This is best served with Crushed Pumpkin (see page 167).

Serves 4 as a main course or 8–10 as a nibble

500g chicken or duck livers, trimmed
*   and patted dry*
1 tsp salt
3 tbsp ghee or clarified butter
1 large onion, finely chopped
2 garlic cloves, finely chopped
4 tbsp pomegranate molasses
2 tbsp lemon juice
½ red chilli, finely chopped
a handful of pomegranate seeds,
*   to garnish*
a handful of chopped flat-leaf parsley,
*   to garnish*

Season the chicken livers with the salt. Heat the ghee in a shallow frying pan over a medium heat, add the chicken livers and sauté for 2 minutes, then flip them over and sauté for 2 minutes on the other side.

Add the onion and garlic, stir and cook for a further minute. Reduce the heat to low and stir in the pomegranate molasses, lemon juice and chilli. Cook for another 30 seconds.

Garnish with pomegranate seeds and chopped flat-leaf parsley. If serving as a main course, serve with crushed pumpkin (see page 167), a big salad, naan bread and natural yoghurt.

CHICKEN MEATBALLS
WITH A QUICK AROMATIC SAUCE

This dish is definitely a favourite with children and I suggest you make large quantities that can be frozen for another day. The addition of Cheddar cheese and breadcrumbs keeps the little balls moist and very tasty. The blend of chicken thigh and breast meat also improves the texture. I like to serve them over crushed boiled potatoes and wilted spinach with a good sprinkling of Dukkah (see page 230).

Serves 6

3 slices of wholemeal bread,
    crusts removed
400g chicken thighs, minced (ideally
    using a mincer but otherwise in a
    food processor)
200g chicken breast, cut into small dice
1 small onion, finely chopped
3 garlic cloves, finely chopped
100g Cheddar cheese (preferably
    aged), grated
2 eggs
2 tbsp wholegrain mustard
4 tbsp chopped flat-leaf parsley

Sauce
4 tbsp olive oil
1 onion, finely chopped
2 garlic cloves, chopped
100g chestnut mushrooms, sliced
1 x 400g can good-quality
    chopped tomatoes
2 tbsp ketchup
3 tbsp soy sauce
2 tbsp HP Brown Sauce
1 tbsp chopped tarragon

Preheat the oven to 200°C/fan 180°C/Gas 6.

Make the sauce. Heat the olive oil over a medium heat in a frying pan and gently sweat the onions until golden brown, then add the garlic. Stir, then add all the remaining ingredients. Transfer to a small saucepan and simmer for 15 minutes.

Meanwhile, place the bread in a bowl with 50ml of water and use the back of a fork to break it down into a purée. Add the remaining ingredients (but only add half the parsley), then mix thoroughly for a couple of minutes.

Lightly wet your hands and shape the mixture into little balls (about the size of large cherry tomatoes).

Lightly oil an ovenproof dish and place the meatballs inside. Place in the oven for 3 minutes to start to set, then remove from the oven and pour over the sauce. Place the dish on the hob over a low heat. Simmer for 5 minutes, mixing gently with a wooden spoon.

Serve sprinkled with the remaining parsley over crushed potatoes, pasta or roast vegetables.

BRUNO'S TIPS

If you make balls of about 180g and flatten them to a burger shape you can cook them on the barbecue – you should get about 4 or 5 chicken burgers.

PAN-FRIED GREY BREAM FILLET ON PISTOU

Pistou is a Provençal vegetable soup, finished with a basil purée (also called a pistou, confusingly). One of my wife's aunts is originally from Marseille and aside from her fun and flamboyant personality, her cooking was another big charm. Every single day of her married life, she cooked two meals a day – to the great satisfaction of her family. The love and happiness she put into her cooking was an inspiration. I remember her telling me that she never followed recipes but cooked with her soul! Her pistou was the best I have ever tasted and it was a celebration of her fantastic vegetable garden. In this dish, I make the pistou soup with less liquid than usual so that it is quite thick, and with the addition of mussels, it makes a great accompaniment to the bream. I suggest you serve it with a dollop of Rouille Sauce (see page 231) as you would for a bouillabaisse and you will get the perfect hybrid Provençal dish.

Serves 6

80g fresh borlotti beans or
    40g dried borlotti
1 bay leaf
1kg mussels
50ml white wine
6 grey bream fillets, about 150g each,
    with skin
25ml olive oil
6 rosemary sprigs
2 tomatoes, deseeded and diced
½ tsp marjoram leaves
salt and black pepper

Pistou
50g bunch of basil
1 garlic clove
50ml olive oil
2 slices of white bread, crusts removed

Soup
25ml olive oil
2 garlic cloves, chopped
200g leeks, diced
150g carrots, diced
1 onion, diced
150g potatoes, diced
150g turnips, diced
150g courgettes, diced
100g green beans, cut into 1cm pieces
100g shelled broad beans

If using dried borlotti beans, soak the beans overnight in five times their volume of cold water.

The next day place the soaked beans in a pan. Cover with cold water, add the bay leaf, bring to the boil then simmer for 45 minutes, until tender.

Soak the mussels in plenty of cold water for 30 minutes. Scrub them clean, then remove the beards (the fibrous clumps attached to the mussels). Discard any that are cracked, broken or remain open when tapped. Drain the mussels in a colander and rinse well.

Heat the white wine in a large pan over a high heat until simmering, add the mussels and cover with a lid. Cook for 4–5 minutes, or until the mussels have opened (discard any that haven't), then remove them from their shells and pass the juice through a fine sieve set over a bowl.

Preheat the oven to 220°C/fan 200°C/Gas 7. For the soup, heat the olive oil in a large pan over a low heat. Add the garlic and stir, then add the leeks, carrots, onion, potatoes, turnips and fresh borlotti, if using. Season very lightly and sweat, stirring often, for 5 minutes, then add the cooked borlotti, if using, and pour in enough water just to cover. Bring to the boil, skim the surface and simmer gently for 15 minutes.

Cover with a lid. Return to the boil, then add the courgettes, green beans and broad beans. Boil gently for 5 minutes then remove from the heat and add the mussels and the strained cooking juices.

Meanwhile, make the pistou. Place all the ingredients in a blender and blend until smooth.

Cook the fish. Line a baking tray with greaseproof paper. Season the fish on both sides with salt and pepper. Heat the olive oil over a high heat in a large frying pan until very hot, then add the seasoned bream, skin-side down. Place a rosemary sprig on top of each piece of fish and lower the heat to medium. After 2 minutes check the skin, it should be golden brown. If so, remove the fish from the pan using a palette knife or fish slice and place on the lined baking tray, skin-side up.

Place the fish in the oven to finish the cooking – it will only take 2–3 minutes so watch it carefully, then remove from the oven. Reheat the soup gently, then add the pistou, tomatoes and marjoram to it and stir well.

To serve, ladle the vegetables and soup liquid into large soup bowls and place a fish fillet on top of each serving. Serve immediately.

BRUNO'S TIPS

I add a bit of bread to the pistou purée to thicken it and give the sauce more texture.

• • •

If you want to save time you can buy frozen broad beans. To prepare, cover the beans with hot water from the tap and leave for 2 minutes, then drain and peel the shells by squeezing them between your fingers – the beans will pop out.

• • •

You can also use a 400g can of borlotti beans. Drain and rinse well. They will need to be added to the soup with the courgettes and green beans.

• • •

The bream could be substituted for salmon or sea trout.

TROUT FILLET WITH SMOKED COD'S ROE CRUST & WILTED SPINACH

My father was a very keen trout fisherman and the wild trout he used to catch were delicious. My mother used to cook them in a frying pan with a bit of vegetable oil then the oil was discarded and replaced with a generous amount of butter and a handful of flaked almonds, a handful of chopped parsley and a little chopped garlic with a dash of homemade wine vinegar to cut through it. With such an amazing ingredient, less is more and the trout needed very little to bring out its fantastic flavour. In the recipe below I use a common rainbow trout; the smoked roe crust will make it a bit more interesting. You could also use sea trout.

Serves 4

80g smoked cod's roe
120g butter, softened
4 slices of white bread,
    crusts removed
4 tbsp dried breadcrumbs
4 tbsp chopped flat-leaf parsley
2 garlic cloves, chopped
1 tsp grated fresh horseradish
2 tbsp lemon juice
4 rainbow trout, about 250–300g
    each, skinned and filleted (you
    can ask your fishmonger to do
    this for you)
4 tbsp olive oil
4 large handfuls spinach
salt and black pepper
1 lemon, quartered, to serve

Place the cod's roe, butter, bread, breadcrumbs, parsley, garlic, horseradish and lemon juice in a food processor and process to a fine paste. Check the seasoning. Remove the paste from the bowl, using a plastic spatula to make sure you scoop it all out, and place on a plate in the fridge for 10 minutes to firm up a bit.

Place a piece of greaseproof paper on a work surface and spread the paste to 1cm thick, then cover with another sheet of paper and roll it out with a rolling pin to 4mm thick. Place on a tray in the fridge for 15 minutes.

Preheat the grill to high. Remove the paste from the fridge and mark out eight rectangles the size of the fish fillets. Peel off the top sheet of paper then roughly cut out and separate each rectangle. Place the exposed pieces of paste on to each fillet, pressing down firmly as you do, then peel off the paper. Trim off any excess paste around the fillet so that each is neatly covered, then transfer the fillets to a non-stick baking tray. Place under the grill. The topping will start to melt and form a crust over the fish. It will cook very fast, in less than 10 minutes, so keep an eye on it.

Meanwhile, heat the olive oil in a frying pan. Add the spinach, season with salt and pepper, then stir with a wooden spoon to wilt.

To serve, divide the spinach between the plates, then place two fillets on each plate, alongside it, accompanied by a lemon quarter. Serve immediately.

BRUNO'S TIPS

I suggest you buy fresh horseradish root (around 200g) rather than the pre-packaged horseradish in jars. Peel and cut it into 4cm pieces, then wrap these individually in cling film and freeze. You can grate the pieces from frozen when you need to and return them to the freezer. This way you will get the full flavour of the root. I actually pick mine on Wimbledon Common!

SAUTEED GURNARD
WITH FENNEL & CITRUS SAUCE

Aside from its culinary uses, gurnard is a very interesting fish. Also called sea robin, it has large pectoral fins, which when opened look like wings. It also has six sort-of-spiny 'legs' and a squareish solid skull. And to top this off, when caught, it sometimes makes a croaking noise a bit like a frog. But what I like most about this fish is its texture: firm but tender, perfect for roasting or braising as a whole fish or simply pan-fried as fillets. The sauce in this dish is easy to make and would go well with other fish.

Serves 4

4 fennel bulbs
2 tbsp clear honey
juice of ½ lemon
5 tbsp olive oil
1 star anise, crushed
1 tbsp rosemary
700g gurnard fillets (see Bruno's Tips)
2 pink grapefruits, segmented
salt and black pepper
Greek basil or very small basil leaves,
  to garnish

Emulsion
300ml freshly squeezed orange juice
80ml olive oil
juice of ¼ lemon

Preheat the oven to 200°C/fan 180°C/Gas 6. Cut each fennel into three or four thick slices, making sure all the layers are attached to the base. Pour the honey, lemon juice, 2 tablespoons of the olive oil and some seasoning into a bowl, whisk well, then add the fennel. Toss so that the fennel slices are coated, then remove and pat dry (reserve the marinade).

Heat a frying pan and colour the fennel on all sides over a high heat, then arrange them side by side in an ovenproof dish. Add 100ml of water and the star anise, then pour over the fennel marinade. Cover with foil and place in the oven for 30 minutes or until soft. The liquid should have evaporated; if not, place the dish on the hob over a medium heat and reduce the liquid to a glaze to coat the fennel slices. Set aside covered with the foil.

For the emulsion, place the orange juice in a pan and reduce by about two thirds, so that you are left with 100ml.

Put the remaining 3 tablespoons of olive oil and the rosemary in a frying pan and fry the gurnard fillets on both sides. When nearly cooked, add 6 tablespoons of water, cover with a lid and leave to rest in the pan for 3–4 minutes (see Bruno's Tips).

Reheat the orange juice, pour into a blender, add the juices from the pan and the 80ml olive oil. Blend on a high speed to obtain a smooth emulsion with a creamy orange colour. Taste and add a squeeze of lemon juice, if needed.

To serve, divide the fennel between the plates, then top with the grapefruit segments, the fish fillets and basil. Pour the orange sauce around.

BRUNO'S TIPS

When buying the gurnard, ask your fishmonger to give you the heads and bones so that you can freeze them. You could use them to make a fish soup or stock (see Bouillabaisse, page 127).

• • •

It is important to leave the fish to 'relax' after frying. Gurnard has quite a compact flesh so this allows it to soften a little, and adding the water keeps it moist. It will release some lovely juices into the pan and become more tender.

SALMON CONFIT WITH ASPARAGUS, NEW POTATOES & GREEN GAZPACHO

If asked to name three savoury ingredients that make them think of an English summer, I bet many people would come up with salmon, asparagus and new potatoes. Usually they will be served with mayonnaise, maybe even with the addition of crème fraîche. I developed this cold soup recipe for a 'green gazpacho' when I lived in Queensland and I thought it would marry well with those ingredients. I tried it on my first summer back in England in my garden, with a Pimm's and some friends and it was quite simply majestic.

Serves 4

4 salmon fillets, about 170g each,
    with skin
1 tsp grated lemon zest
1 tsp rosemary leaves
400ml olive oil
24 small new potatoes
16 green asparagus spears, peeled
    at the stalk end
celery salt and black pepper

Gazpacho
4 tsp olive oil
1 tbsp cider vinegar
1 tsp natural yoghurt
100g cucumber
1 spring onion
¼ green pepper
⅛ avocado
½ tsp finely chopped green chilli
½ garlic clove
4 basil leaves
3 mint leaves
salt and black pepper
3 pinches of sugar

You will also need a cooking thermometer

Marinate the salmon at least 2 hours before cooking. Place the fillets on a plate flesh-side up and season with the lemon zest, rosemary, celery salt and pepper. Cover with cling film and refrigerate for 2 hours.

Pour the olive oil into a pan or ovenproof dish that will hold the four fillets snugly. Heat the oil very slowly to 50°C, regulating the temperature by using a cooking thermometer. Keep the temperature between 50 and 55°C throughout the cooking. Place the salmon in the oil, skin-side down, then adjust the temperature to 50°C again to cook it. It will take about 30 minutes to slow-cook (confit) the salmon.

Meanwhile, place the potatoes in boiling salted water and cook until tender but not soft, about 8–10 minutes. Drain and keep warm.

For the gazpacho, first put the oil, cider vinegar and yoghurt into a blender, then add the remaining ingredients and two ice cubes (these will keep the soup cold during the processing). Blend until smooth, then check the seasoning and pass through a fine sieve. Transfer to a sauce boat or jug for serving and chill until ready to serve.

When ready to eat, plunge the asparagus into salted boiling water for about 2 minutes, then drain in a colander. Divide the asparagus and new potatoes between serving plates. Using a palette knife, carefully lift the salmon out of the cooking oil (see Bruno's Tips) and place on kitchen paper to absorb any excess oil, then place alongside the vegetables. Pour over a little of the gazpacho, then serve the rest in the sauce boat for everybody to help themselves, or I think it is quite fun to serve the gazpacho in small glasses to drink as you eat.

BRUNO'S TIPS

The cooking oil can be passed through a fine sieve then placed in a sterilised jar in the fridge so that you can re-use it, either to make the confit again or to pan-fry fish.

• • •

I usually finish the dish with some lightly dressed fresh garden herbs.

STAFF DINNER PORK RIBS

I have cooked this dish as a staff meal for many years. In general everyone loves it and asks for the recipe. It is perfect for a summer barbecue but it can also be cooked in the oven on rainy days.

It's funny because at the time of writing we have decided to cook only vegetarian meals for the staff at Bistrot Bruno Loubet and the Zetter Hotel. This is due to different religions, tastes and cultures. Cooking food for 60 people twice a day can be difficult and it seems to be the unwanted daily task in the kitchen, but on the occasions I do it I really enjoy it. I often say to my chefs, if you don't enjoy cooking for your colleagues and don't even respect your own meal, how can you make it a profession and cook for customers? Cooking is about giving the best of yourself and feeling proud of what you've done.

Serves 6

2.5kg meaty pork ribs, separated
50ml vegetable oil

Marinade
2 tbsp creamed horseradish
3 tbsp dark soy sauce
6 tbsp ketchup
3 tbsp Worcestershire sauce
2 tbsp grated fresh root ginger
2 garlic cloves, chopped
1 tsp grated orange zest
2 tbsp tomato purée
1 tbsp honey
6 tbsp red wine vinegar
1 tsp smoked paprika
2 tsp Tabasco chipotle sauce
black pepper

Preheat the oven 200°C/fan 180°C/ Gas 6.

Place all the ingredients for the marinade in a bowl and mix well with a spoon. Brush generously over the ribs then lay them in a roasting tin and drizzle over the oil. Spoon over any remaining marinade.

Place the tin in the oven for about 45 minutes. You will need to roll the ribs in the sauce a few times during the cooking to achieve a nice glaze. If after 45 minutes the ribs are cooked but the sauce is not glazing the ribs enough, place over a medium heat on the hob to reduce the sauce quickly. Keep rolling the ribs when you are doing this until the sauce looks sticky. Serve immediately.

BRUNO'S TIPS

I suggest you serve the ribs with roast potatoes and a nice bowl of mixed leaf salad or steamed bok choy.

• • •

If you don't fancy holding bones and working your teeth on the ribs, use lean pork belly for this recipe. It will cook at a lower temperature (190°C/fan 170°C/ Gas 5) for a longer time – at least an hour.

SWEET SOY BRAISED BEEF CHEEKS
WITH MANGO SALAD

My eight years in Australia were very interesting. Queensland is a hot place and the outdoor life inevitably influences the food. Sometimes I found myself scratching my head in desperation to find an alternative way to cook a dish. The difficulty was adapting a dish without losing the core idea that made it a 'classic'.

When I opened my first restaurant in Brisbane, it was called Bruno's Tables. I decided that everything I served there would be food I loved to eat myself and that I wouldn't make any concessions towards trends or expectations. My first resolution was not to have steak on the menu. This was quite a brave (or uninformed!) move in a city where the quality of a restaurant is too often judged by the quality of its steak!

The idea for this dish came quite easily. I decided to do a braised beef using the best cut for that: cheeks. But beef braised in red wine, as is classic in French cuisine, was too rich and potentially boring for Brisbanites who were used to exciting Asian food influences. So I decided to use the classic French technique but change the ingredients. I braised the cheeks with sweet Indonesian soy sauce, lemon grass and Kaffir lime leaves that grew in my garden, and local ginger. The usual mashed vegetables gave way to a local mango and herb salad. The dish was an instant hit and has become a classic in its own right. The unusual salad served with the braised meat always seemed to surprise people – even chefs, but when they taste it they are impressed by how well the ingredients work together and how refreshing it is. I served this dish for a dinner celebrating my friend Raymond Blanc's 60th birthday. For me this dish shows how traditions can be adapted to changes in life.

Serves 6

4 tbsp olive oil
2kg beef cheeks, trimmed
300g carrots, sliced
200g celery, sliced
2 onions, diced
5 garlic cloves, crushed
a 5cm piece of fresh root
    ginger, sliced
1 star anise
1 lemon grass stalk, crushed
3 tbsp pomegranate molasses
9 tbsp sweet Indonesian soy sauce
    (Kecap manis)
2 tbsp sweet chilli sauce
3 Kaffir lime leaves, bruised
500ml veal or beef stock
3 green cardamom pods, crushed
grated zest of 1 orange, plus 1 long
    piece of peel
3 tbsp lime juice
toasted sesame seeds, to garnish

Salad

1 mango, peeled and sliced
12 spring onions, finely sliced
½ cucumber, finely sliced
3 tbsp roughly chopped mint
3 tbsp roughly chopped coriander
4 tbsp roughly chopped basil
wedge of lime, to serve

Dressing

4 tbsp sesame oil
1 tbsp sweet chilli sauce
1 garlic clove
1 tsp chopped fresh root ginger
1 Kaffir lime leaf, very
    finely chopped
50ml olive oil
3 tbsp lime juice
1 tsp palm sugar

Preheat the oven to the oven to 220°C/fan 200°C/Gas 7.

Heat the oil in a frying pan and colour the beef on all sides, then remove with tongs or a slotted spoon and set aside. In the same pan, place the carrots, celery and onions and fry gently over a medium heat until golden brown.

Place the beef in a casserole or heavy ovenproof dish, add the vegetables and all the remaining ingredients. Add enough water to cover the cheeks with 3cm of liquid above the meat. Place a circle of greaseproof paper on top, then an old plate, which will keep the beef submerged. Cover the dish with the lid, or if you don't have a lid use a double layer of foil. Place in the oven for 3 hours. Check whether the beef is ready by squeezing a piece of meat between two fingers. It should feel like your fingers would go through it and break it if you pushed hard. Leave the meat to rest in the sauce for at least 30 minutes or it will dry out.

Using a slotted spoon, remove the meat from the sauce, place in a dish and cover with cling film to prevent it from drying out. Pass the sauce through a fine sieve over a clean pan, then bring to the boil and skim the surface. Leave to reduce to a nice rich sauce consistency, then turn off the heat and add the meat.

To make the dressing, place all the ingredients in a blender and blend until smooth.

Make the salad by mixing all the ingredients in a bowl then add the dressing.

To serve, place a mound of salad on one side of each plate with the beef and sauce on the other. Sprinkle with toasted sesame seeds and serve immediately.

BRUNO'S TIPS

Because the time involved in the preparation is quite long, I suggest you cook the meat the day before (it will only improve in flavour), leaving you simply to finish off the sauce and the salad on the day. The meat can be reheated in the sauce over a low heat on the hob.

GUINEA FOWL OR FREE-RANGE CHICKEN ROASTED WITH GARLIC & PARSLEY PUREE UNDER THE SKIN

This dish is one of my favourite ways to eat guinea fowl or chicken. Based on a recipe of my mother's, I used to serve it when working at the Four Seasons Hotel in Park Lane in London, which was then called Inn on the Park. Mr Ramón Pajares was the general manager and working with him was such a privilege. I was quite young for the position at the time but he was always there for me, listening to my problems and frustrations and pushing me to cook what I believed in, trusting me fully. This freedom gave me the confidence to put dishes on the menu that no one would have expected to find in a luxury hotel restaurant. It was a calculated risk taken by Mr Pajares, but one that resulted in great success as we achieved a Michelin star within a year.

Serves 4

300ml dark chicken stock
1 guinea fowl or chicken, about 1.5kg
4 tbsp olive oil
4 tbsp yoghurt
salt and black pepper

Garlic butter
10 garlic cloves, crushed
2 large handfuls of flat-leaf
* parsley leaves*
125g butter, softened
salt and black pepper

Stuffing
30g butter
200g chicken livers, trimmed
* and patted dry*
1 onion, finely chopped
100g smoked streaky bacon,
* very finely chopped*
4 tbsp dried breadcrumbs
1 egg

First, place the chicken stock in a small pan and bubble to reduce it by half and concentrate the flavours.

To make the garlic butter, blanch the garlic and the parsley in boiling salted water for 30 seconds, then drain and place in cold water to cool. Drain and squeeze out any excess water, then place in a food processor with the soft butter and seasoning and process until the parsley turns the butter a lovely green colour. Spoon the green butter into a piping bag and set aside.

For the stuffing, heat the butter in a frying pan until foaming, then add the chicken livers. Cook for 30 seconds on each side, then remove the livers to a plate and place the pan back on the heat. Add the onion, then reduce the heat to low to cook slowly until soft and lightly coloured. At this stage add the bacon and give it a good mix. Pour the mixture into a mixing bowl and add the breadcrumbs and egg. Chop the livers finely then add to the bowl and mix thoroughly to combine. Divide the mixture into four and shape into balls.

Preheat the oven to 200°C/fan 180°C/ Gas 6.

Take the guinea fowl, and starting from the hole at the neck, slide your fingers gently under the skin of the breast to detach it from the flesh, then push around the leg. Push the piping bag under the skin as far as the legs then pipe the butter under the skin, pulling the bag back over the breast towards you. Repeat the operation on the other side of the bird, then with your hands, press and move the skin to spread the butter evenly.

Brush the guinea fowl all over with the olive oil, season lightly with salt and pepper then place in a roasting tin, breast-side up, and roast in the oven for 15 minutes. Baste it with the tin juices, then place the stuffing balls around the bird and return to the oven for another 15–20 minutes.

Remove the tin from the oven, cut off the legs and return the bird to the oven for a further 10 minutes. Check the bird is cooked by pricking the leg with a skewer to check whether the juices run clear.

To serve, cut the legs into two. Remove the breasts and cut in half. On each serving plate, place a piece of breast, a piece of leg and a ball of stuffing, lightly crushed with the back of a spoon. Mix the hot cooking juices with the yoghurt and the reduced stock (see Bruno's Tips). Stir well and pour all over the meat.

BRUNO'S TIPS

The advice usually given in recipes is to baste chicken with its dripping regularly. In this recipe you will only need to do it twice at the most because the butter between the skin and flesh will melt, giving the bird moisture and extra flavour. The lovely green under the skin will create a background for the gorgeous dark golden skin and the stuffing gives and takes flavours from the bird. This technique can also be applied to turkey and quail.

• • •

For me, roasted potatoes and a large bowl of mixed leaves are unbeatable with this dish.

• • •

You may need to add a drop of good-quality sherry vinegar to the cooking juices to adjust the acidity.

GRILLED MARINATED QUAIL, BROAD BEAN, QUINOA & TREVISO SALAD

Quinoa is a South American grain packed with nutrients that is currently enjoying a renaissance in the food world. Its nutritional value was recognised by the Incas and as such it was dubbed the 'mother seed' and was sacred. The slight nutty, almost creamy flavour and the fluffy texture make it a great alternative to couscous or bulgur wheat.

Quails cooked on the barbecue are delicious and should be eaten with your fingers for maximum enjoyment. I think this is the perfect summer dish.

Serves 4

6 large quails, cut in half lengthways

Marinade
1 tsp chopped garlic
1 tsp grated lemon zest
4 tbsp olive oil
1 tbsp clear honey
1 tbsp lemon juice
1 tbsp rosemary leaves
salt and black pepper

Salad
300g quinoa
6 tbsp olive oil
2 tbsp good-quality red wine vinegar
25ml apple juice
6 lovage leaves
6 spring onions, sliced
350g shelled and skinned broad beans
¼ head of Treviso lettuce, trimmed and shredded

First, marinate the quail. Mix all the ingredients for the marinade in a shallow dish and rub all over the quail. Cover with cling film and place in the fridge for at least 1 hour.

Cook the quinoa in plenty of boiling water for about 9 minutes, or until cooked.

Place the olive oil, vinegar, apple juice and lovage in a blender and blitz until smooth.

When cooked, drain the quinoa, then place in a bowl. While still hot, pour the lovage dressing over and mix well. Add the spring onions, broad beans and shredded Treviso but wait to mix the salad until the quail is cooked.

Heat a griddle pan over a medium heat until hot, then add the quail skin-side down and cook for 3 minutes, then flip over and cook for 2 minutes on the flesh side. Reduce the heat to low, and finish cooking the quail slowly for 5 minutes, until the meat is no longer pink but still juicy.

To serve, mix the salad, divide between the serving plates and place three quail halves on each serving.

BRUNO'S TIPS

Place paper napkins and individual finger bowls with a slice of lemon in front of each guest and encourage everyone to use their fingers. This recipe will also work well with spatchcocked poussin.

SUSTAINABLE BOUILLABAISSE

Where do I start? This is such an iconic dish from Marseille. It is said to have originated in the creeks around the city. Fishermen coming back from the sea would make their meal out of unsellable fish boiled in seawater then poured over sliced bread rubbed with garlic. I imagine that whoever made it must have had their own version cooked with a few Provençal herbs, spices or tomatoes.

Today, bouillabaisse is traditionally a rich, fragrant fish soup garnished with different rockfish. To give some 'nobility' to the dish a group of Provençal restaurateurs defend its appellation with regulated standards.

In Provence, bouillabaisse often has to be ordered with 24 hours' notice so that the right fish can be purchased. I fully respect this and sincerely believe it's great for the dish and the region, but for me in London – or rather, for my customers – this doesn't work. Also, as with many other chefs, sustainability has become part of my ethos; I simply can't ignore the future of my children and grandchildren. And it all starts with what we buy. Climate change and food sustainability are two major issues for the future of humankind and within that the future of our fish supply is one of the biggest causes of concern. Overfishing, wastage and a disregard for seasonality – the mating season in particular – means that we are in danger of losing some of our fish species altogether. So if you're not already a sustainable fish supporter, I'd urge you, please, to make it your mission to buy conscientiously. It can be a confusing and sometimes difficult path to navigate but there are very good resources available to help you, including the Marine Stewardship Council website (www.msc.org).

This is a special dish that cannot be made in small quantities to savour the experience fully, so the recipe below is for eight.

Serves 8

1 fennel
250g leeks, sliced
16 new potatoes, peeled and boiled
2 pinches of saffron threads
600g gurnard, cut into
    large chunks
500g sea bream
500g mackerel fillets
800g mussels, cleaned and debearded
8 raw tiger prawns, peeled but
    with head and tail still on
100g tomatoes, diced
1 handful of small basil leaves
(optional)
Rouille Sauce (see page 231),
    to serve
40 slices of baguette, toasted,
    to serve

Soup base

8 tbsp olive oil
200g carrots, peeled and finely sliced
150g leeks, trimmed and finely sliced
250g onions, finely sliced
5 garlic cloves, chopped
1 star anise
½ tsp coriander seeds, toasted
    and crushed
5 cardamom pods, crushed
½ chilli, chopped
zest of ¼ orange
500g whiting bones and trimmings
700g gurnard bones and trimmings
500g sea bream bones and trimmings
600g sole or plaice bones
200ml white wine
1 x 400g can good-quality
    chopped tomatoes
2 tbsp tomato purée
1 tsp dried Provençal herbs
salt and black pepper

Start by making the soup base. Preheat the oven to 220°C/fan 200°C/ Gas 7. Put half the olive oil in a large pan and sweat the carrots, leeks, onions, garlic, star anise, coriander seeds, cardamom, chilli and orange zest over a medium heat, stirring from time to time to avoid colouration.

Meanwhile, place all the fish bones, head or trimmings in a roasting tin with the remaining olive oil and place in the oven for 6–8 minutes to set the proteins.

Add the white wine to the vegetables, bring to a vigorous boil and boil for 30 seconds, then add the chopped tomatoes and tomato purée and stir well. Add the cooked fish bones, then cover them with 5cm of cold water. Increase the heat and bring to the

boil, then lower the heat and skim the surface. Now you can add the Provençal herbs. Leave to simmer for an hour, stirring from time to time and making sure you scrape the bottom of the pan otherwise the vegetables could catch. Check the liquid level in the pan and add more water if necessary. After an hour, the fish bones should be very soft and beginning to break down.

Pass the soup liquid through a colander set over another pan and keep aside. With a potato masher, mash the vegetables and bones as much as you can, then pour the cooking liquid back into the pan.

Pass the mixture through a fine sieve or colander, then pass it a second time through a fine sieve, pressing down with a small ladle or a large spoon to extract as much liquid as possible.

Put the soup in a clean pot to use as a base for cooking the vegetable garnish. Add the fennel and bring the liquid to the boil, then lower the heat and simmer for 10 minutes. Add the leeks, potatoes and saffron, return to a simmer and cook for another 10 minutes, then lower the heat and leave to simmer gently for another 10 minutes. The soup is now ready to receive the pieces of fish.

About 20 minutes before serving, add the gurnard and leave to simmer slowly for 3 minutes, then add the sea bream, mackerel, mussels and prawns and leave to simmer for another 3 minutes. Add the diced tomatoes and scatter over the basil leaves, if using. Check the seasoning.

Remove from the heat and serve it within the next 10–15 minutes with the Rouille Sauce and toasted baguette.

BRUNO'S TIPS

When buying the fish for the soup, ask your fishmonger to fillet it for you but to set aside all the bones and heads for you so that you can use them for the soup base. Ask the fishmonger to give you some extra sole or plaice bones.

MY FATHER'S COTE DE BOEUF

In winter, after the pruning of the grapevines, all the cuttings are put together in bundles. When I was a child we used to do our own and store them in the garden shed. The Bordeaux region has a great tradition of cooking ribs of beef or other cuts of meat on embers made from the vine cuttings, as they give the most delicious smoky and nutty flavours. My father used to have his own way of cooking this dish, which in turn became our family tradition when we had friends over. A charcoal barbecue can of course be used instead – it will still be very good.

Serves 4

120g shallots, finely chopped
2 garlic cloves, finely chopped
1 tbsp white wine vinegar
120g bone marrow
1.2kg rib of beef
salt and black pepper

Place the shallots, garlic and some seasoning in a small bowl. Mix well with a spoon, pressing the shallots against the sides of the bowl. This will help the shallots to soften on the meat during cooking.

In a small saucepan, heat 200ml of water with the vinegar and 4 pinches of salt. When boiling, remove from the heat and add the bone marrow. Leave the marrow in the water for 30 seconds then lift out of the water and place on a small plate.

Heat a wood or charcoal barbecue until hot. Season the beef rib and sear on all sides, then cook on the largest side for 4 minutes. Turn it to cook the other large side and spread the shallot mixture over. Leave for another 2 minutes. This will give you a rare piece of meat. For meat that's more cooked see Bruno's Tips. Remove from the barbecue and lay the rib on a wooden chopping board in a warm place for 3½ minutes to rest, then slice at the table.

BRUNO'S TIPS

You could add 2 tablespoons of whisky to the shallots when adding the salt – I have discovered that it brings an even more smoky flavour to the dish. I am sure that my father would have approved.

• • •

Serve with ceps if you can get your hands on them or a selection of wild mushrooms cooked in the same way (see my recipe for Cèpes à la Bordelaise on page 177). Serve with sautéed potatoes and a mixed leaf salad.

• • •

If you like your rib more cooked, lower the heat and close the barbecue top until it is cooked to your taste.

WILD PIGEON
WITH RAW & COOKED CAULIFLOWER & BLACKBERRY SAUCE

When talking about pigeons, Londoners can't help but associate them with Trafalgar Square and think of them as 'flying rats' – a pest in their great city. Rest assured the pigeons you will find at your butcher are wild; they come from the countryside and have been shot in open fields where they have been treating themselves to lovely food from our farmers. By eating them we participate in maintaining the agricultural balance. Wild pigeon is sustainable, abundant and delicious.

Wild blackberries are so much better than cultivated ones (they make my favourite flavour of jam), so if you can forage for your blackberries on a day out, this sauce will be even better.

Serves 6

9 oven-ready wild pigeons
12 juniper berries, crushed
2 tbsp vegetable oil
150g shallots
1 parsnip, finely sliced
3 garlic cloves
1 bay leaf
5 sprigs of fresh thyme
200ml port
50ml brandy
500ml veal stock or dark chicken stock
500ml milk
½ tsp caraway seeds
1 large cauliflower, cut into florets
80g butter
150ml walnut oil
50ml good-quality red wine vinegar
2 tbsp chopped chives
120g wild blackberries, lightly crushed
2 tbsp olive oil
salt and black pepper

Preheat the oven to 240°C/fan 220°C/ Gas 9.

Using a sharp knife, cut the breasts off the pigeons, leaving the skin covering them. Season the breasts with salt, pepper and crushed juniper.

Rinse the pigeon carcasses under water, then dry them well. Place in a roasting tray with the vegetable oil, then place in the hot oven and cook for 4–5 minutes, until light brown. Remove from the oven, lift out the bones and place in a saucepan.

Add 100g of the shallots, the parsnip, garlic, bay leaf and thyme to the roasting tin. Place the tin over a medium heat on the hob to colour the vegetables, stirring with a spoon.

When the shallots and parsnip are lightly browned, add the port and brandy and increase the heat to bring to a vigorous boil. Use a wooden spoon to scrape the bottom of the pan to deglaze it and detach all the caramelised residue. Pour all the liquid into the saucepan with the bones, then add the stock and enough water to cover the bones with 5cm of liquid. Bring to the boil, skimming the surface, then reduce the heat and leave to simmer for 1 hour.

Meanwhile, prepare your garnish. Place the milk in a pan with the caraway seeds and some salt and bring to the boil. Add half the cauliflower florets and simmer until soft – this will take about 20 minutes.

Drain the milk over a bowl and place the cauliflower in a food processor with 50g of the butter and 3 or 4 tablespoons of the cooking milk. Purée until smooth then place in a small pan, ready to be reheated just before serving.

Using a mandoline or very sharp knife, cut the remaining raw cauliflower into very fine slices over a mixing bowl then season with salt, pepper, walnut oil and vinegar. Finely chop the remaining shallots and add them to the bowl along with the chives. Mix well.

Pass the stock through a fine sieve and return to the pan. Bubble and reduce to a light sauce consistency. Skim the top from time to time to clean the sauce of any impurities or scum. Finish with the remaining 30g of butter, swirling the pan to mix,

then add the blackberries to infuse in the sauce. Check the seasoning.

To serve, gently reheat the cauliflower purée. Heat the olive oil in a non-stick frying pan until hot. Season the pigeon breasts, then fry, skin-side down, for 2 minutes, then flip over and cook on the flesh side for a minute (fry them in batches if necessary).

Spoon the hot purée on to a plate, then add three breasts and scatter over the raw cauliflower. Finish with the sauce.

BRUNO'S TIPS

This recipe will be a lot less time-consuming on the day if you make the sauce the day before.

MY SPAGHETTI BORDELAISE

My daughters love spaghetti Bolognese and so do I. One Sunday, years ago, some friends dropped by for a late afternoon drink and my wife invited them to stay for dinner (as she usually does) and said *we'd* cook a nice meal. Let me explain: in these impromptu situations, 'we' means me. So 'we' look in the fridge to find out that spaghetti Bolognese had been planned for that night, so I decided to glamorise it a little, to the great appreciation of all. 'We' just created a new dish! The fair amount of red wine added in this recipe makes it 'Bordelaise' for me!

Serves 6

3 tbsp olive oil
100g pancetta, cut into fine strips or dice
250g Toulouse sausage, skinned and
    broken up
400g minced beef
150g carrots, peeled and finely chopped
100g celery, finely chopped
1 red pepper, finely chopped
1 onion, finely chopped
4 garlic cloves, chopped
1 tbsp dried Provençal herbs
300ml red wine
1 x 400g can good-quality
    chopped tomatoes
1 tbsp tomato purée
2 tbsp Worcestershire sauce
⅓ tsp smoked paprika
500g spaghetti
60g butter
2 tbsp finely chopped flat-leaf
    parsley leaves
salt and black pepper
80g Manchego cheese, grated, to serve

Heat the olive oil in a frying pan, add the pancetta, stir well and cook for 2–3 minutes over a medium heat.

Add the sausage and minced beef. Stir from time to time to fry all the meat evenly then pour it all in a colander set over a dish to save all the drippings. Mix well with a spoon.

Pour the drippings back in the pan, then add the chopped vegetables, garlic and herbs. Cook for about 10 minutes, stirring from time to time, until the vegetables are a light brown colour, then pour it all into a casserole.

Add the meat and the red wine, bring to the boil and simmer for 2 minutes, then add the tomatoes and the tomato purée, Worcestershire sauce and paprika. Mix well, then cover with a lid and simmer for 45 minutes. Check the seasoning.

Cook the spaghetti according to the packet instructions, then drain and toss with the butter.

To serve, divide the spaghetti between serving plates, spoon the sauce over, and sprinkle with the parsley. Serve with the Manchego cheese alongside for everyone to help themselves.

BRUNO'S TIPS

Too often I feel that Bolognese sauces are not cooked for long enough to build up the depth of flavour, so make sure you cook it for the full 45 minutes.

• • •

You can save time by pulsing the vegetables in the food processor to chop them. Just be careful you make them a size similar to lentils and don't mash them.

WILD RABBIT, PLUM & JERUSALEM ARTICHOKE TAGINE

The English countryside is home to plenty of rabbits, making them a sustainable and reasonably priced meat; two good reasons to eat them.

They are also very tasty, usually braised to tenderise the meat, and they will produce a great sauce. This recipe is inspired by North African cuisine and the sauce is quite light, more like a gamey broth with underlying layers of soft spices and dried fruits.

Serves 4

3 tbsp olive oil
1kg wild rabbit, jointed into pieces
    (you can ask your butcher to do this)
200g shallots, sliced
300g leeks
1 small bay leaf
1 tbsp oregano leaves
4 garlic cloves, sliced
½ green chilli
½ tsp cumin seeds, toasted
⅓ cinnamon stick
2 oranges: pared rind of 1; grated
    zest of the other
400ml dark chicken stock
3 tbsp red wine vinegar
1 tbsp black treacle
1 tsp chopped fresh root ginger
300g Jerusalem artichokes, peeled
    and cut into 3
6 red plums, halved
1 handful of parsley leaves
6 mint leaves
1 handful of young coriander leaves
salt and black pepper
warmed pitta bread, to serve

If you are going to cook this dish in a tagine rather than a casserole, preheat the oven to 200°C/fan 180°C/Gas 6.

Heat the olive oil in a frying pan over a medium heat, add the rabbit pieces and colour on all sides. Lift out the rabbit and set aside, then add the shallots, leek, bay leaf, oregano, garlic, chilli, cumin, cinnamon and pared orange rind to the same pan. Cook over a medium heat until nicely browned, then add the orange zest, chicken stock, rabbit pieces, vinegar, treacle, ginger and Jerusalem artichokes. Pour the mixture into a tagine or a casserole.

If using a casserole, bring to the boil, then lower the heat, skim the top and leave to simmer gently, covered with the lid, for 1 hour. If using a tagine, cover with the lid and bake in the oven for 1½ hours.

After 30 minutes, add the plums. Check the seasoning before serving, then sprinkle over the parsley, mint and coriander. Open the tagine at the table and serve with hot pitta bread.

BRUNO'S TIPS

If you are jointing the rabbit yourself, make sure you use a sharp, heavy knife to avoid any small bits of bone.

• • •

If Jerusalem artichokes are not in season or simply hard to find, I suggest you replace them with sweet potatoes.

• • •

I'd recommend buying a tagine from a North African shop, it looks great for serving and keeps forever. At home I am still using one I bought in Marrakech about 15 years ago.

TURKEY PAUPIETTE
WITH DRIED CRANBERRY SAUCE

Last year my 13-year-old daughter looked at me and said: 'Dad, for Christmas this year, can we have a roast turkey with all the trimmings like everybody else does, for a change?' (which I found very funny). So we did and it was beautiful! Thinking about it, I have to say that she made me realise that there's a stigma attached to cooking turkey – people think it can be dry – and it's a poultry we generally only use at Christmas, which is a shame as it is so versatile. So this recipe is a welcome change, perfect for cooking at any time of the year and a great alternative to a 'dry roast'. A *paupiette* is a classic French dish in which a thin piece of meat, often veal, is stuffed and rolled then cooked in a stock so there's absolutely no risk of it being dry. My favourite accompaniment for this dish is cauliflower cheese.

Serves 6

1kg skinless turkey breast, cut into
    6 thin slices (you can ask your butcher
    to do this for you or see Bruno's Tips)
240g boneless turkey thighs, minced
2 tbsp dried breadcrumbs
50ml white wine
50g butter
1 large onion, finely chopped
180g smoked streaky bacon, minced
4 sage leaves
1 egg, lightly beaten
⅓ tsp freshly grated nutmeg
salt and black pepper

Sauce
1 onion, chopped
100g celery, chopped
1 garlic clove, sliced
3 tbsp cider vinegar
300ml veal or dark chicken stock
100g dried cranberries, soaked in hot
    water for 1 hour then drained
1 tbsp cranberry jelly
80g butter
3 tbsp chopped chives

If you cut the turkey breast yourself and have any trimmings, mince them and add to the minced thigh meat.

Place a piece of cling film on a chopping board. Brush some water over it using a pastry brush, then lay a slice of meat on top. Brush with water again then cover with another piece of film to sandwich it. Tap it with a rolling pin (not too hard), to start breaking up the fibres, then roll it out in all directions to get a thin 5mm slice (an escalope). Repeat with the other five slices.

Preheat the oven to 220°C/fan 200°C/ Gas 7. Soak the breadcrumbs in a bowl with the white wine. With the back of a fork, mash to a purée.

Heat the butter in a small pan, then add the onion and sweat until soft. Pour the onion and butter into the breadcrumb mixture, making sure you scrape out all the butter that is in the pan. Leave to cool for a few minutes, then add all the remaining ingredients to make the stuffing. Mix well with a wooden spoon.

Lay the turkey escalopes out on a work surface, then shape the stuffing mixture into six even balls and place on top of each escalope. Wrap the escalopes around them to form balls, then wrap tightly in a double layer of lightly oiled foil. Transfer to a roasting tin and place in the oven for 15 minutes.

Remove from the oven, then unwrap the foil over the roasting tin to collect any juices and fat and transfer the turkey paupiettes to a plate, cover with cling film and set aside.

To make the sauce, add the onion, celery and garlic to the roasting tin. Place over a medium heat to colour the vegetables, then add the vinegar. Bring to a vigorous boil, then add the stock and the paupiettes. Cover with foil and return to the oven for 10 minutes.

Remove from the oven and place the paupiettes on a serving dish or plates. Pass the sauce through a fine sieve into a small saucepan, then add the cranberries and the jelly. Bubble to reduce it if it looks too thin, then add the butter and heat through.

Swirl the pan for the sauce to absorb the butter, then add the chives. Pour the sauce over the paupiettes and serve immediately.

BRUNO'S TIPS

To cut the turkey breast, place the whole breast on a chopping board. Using a long, thin sharp knife, slice at a 45° angle starting from the top. Cut a slice and repeat to get 6 slices in total.

• • •

If you do want to roast a whole turkey, then I suggest you spike the turkey breast with fatty pieces of bacon dusted with black pepper and a bit of ground cinnamon and also place some butter under the skin (see the method for the Guinea Fowl or Free-range Chicken Roasted with Garlic & Parsley Purée on page 121, but use plain butter instead of the herb butter).

TURKEY & BLUE CHEESE
TRIPLE DECKER CROQUE MONSIEUR

A couple of years ago *Jamie* [Oliver] *Magazine* ran an article on how to use up Christmas leftovers and they asked me to contribute to the piece. I came up with this recipe, which I make at home and everyone still loves it. So much so that I sometimes buy turkey just to make this delicious sandwich on Sunday nights. It's addictive and my wife calls it 'croque monster'!

I think my mother was the expert in food recycling. Nothing, absolutely nothing, went to waste and she had a real talent for making use of leftovers. Leftover beef went into stuffed tomatoes, or leftover meat was stewed with extra caramelised onions and mushrooms that we'd foraged to make an exciting sauce for pasta; leftover vegetables added to a cheese sauce with fresh herbs and mustard always won the hearts of her seven children. She had a gift.

Serves 4

250ml Béchamel Sauce (see page 239)
100g your favourite blue cheese
    (I love Gorgonzola)
1 heaped tbsp Dijon mustard
1 tbsp Worcestershire sauce
8 tsp cranberry sauce
12 slices of wholemeal bread
80g Emmental cheese, grated
400g roast turkey – dark and white
    meat, thinly sliced
salt and black pepper

Preheat the oven to 200°C/fan 180°C/Gas 6.

Place the Béchamel sauce, blue cheese, mustard and Worcestershire sauce in a food processor. Give it a very quick blitz, just enough to mix it well.

Spread the cranberry sauce over eight of the bread slices (only on one side), then cover the cranberry with the Béchamel mixture.

Sprinkle the Emmental on the four slices with no cranberry sauce; they will be the tops of the sandwiches.

Divide the meat between the eight slices with cranberry and Béchamel, then build up four sandwiches, finishing with the Emmental-covered slices. Place on a baking tray in the oven for about 8 minutes, or until the cheese is bubbling and golden and the sandwiches are heated through.

BRUNO'S TIPS

The cranberry sauce can be replaced by piccalilli if you prefer.

• • •

I love to serve this dish with steamed broccoli with a dash of good red wine vinegar over it.

MACKEREL WITH SALTED & COMPRESSED WATERMELON & LIME MAYONNAISE

My mother used to sprinkle melon with a little salt before eating it, something that as a child I found horrible. I often wondered why she did it. And also where the idea came from. I found it intriguing so began to experiment in different ways to try to make sense of it – this recipe is the result of one of those attempts. I salted a piece of watermelon and compressed it in a vacuum. The result was interesting. Not only did it change the flavour but also the texture of the watermelon; it became more 'meaty' with a salty, fruity taste, excellent for pairing with fish or seafood.

Serves 4

250g watermelon
4 small mackerel fillets, with skin
2 tbsp olive oil
4 tbsp mayonnaise
juice of 1 lime
2 tbsp thin chives, cut into 3cm lengths
salt and black pepper

Slice the watermelon into 2cm–thick slices, then sprinkle with salt on both sides. Cut off the skin and discard.

Place the melon between two sheets of cling film on a plate, then cover with another plate and place a 2kg weight on top. Leave for 20 minutes, then cut the melon into dice.

Season the mackerel fillets. Heat a tablespoon of olive oil in a frying pan over a high heat and add the fish skin-side down. When lightly coloured, turn off the heat and turn on to the flesh side. Leave for 20 seconds, then remove from the pan and place on a plate. Mix the mayonnaise with the lime juice.

To serve, place the melon on the plates with the mackerel alongside. Either drizzle or dot the lime mayonnaise over using a teaspoon, or in a squeezy bottle.

Top with the chives to finish. Drizzle with the remaining tablespoon of olive oil and add a crack of pepper.

GRILLED MARINATED CALVES' LIVER
WITH GREEN TOMATO CHUTNEY & POLENTA

I remember going once to *la triperie* (the tripe shop) as a little boy. It was in a little street near the market in Libourne, my home town. My mum pushed open the large metal and glass door. We went in and I remember feeling very intimidated by the clinical aspect of the place, which was covered in white tiles. A huge red-faced man was standing at the counter expertly cutting slice after slice of calves' liver with a long knife. He looked at us and said, 'Bonjour,' and asked my mother what she would like to buy. By that time I'd realised that his long white apron was stained all over with blood. I started to squeeze my mother's hand and was glued to her! My mother said that the liver he was cutting would do: 'Three slices, please'. 'Good choice', the man replied. 'The beast was only slaughtered 24 hours ago.' My mother said, 'I know, that's why I came today,' then looked at me and gave me a wink. I was only a little boy but I understood the lesson. It's all about freshness and provenance, eating food at its best.

Serves 4

Firm Polenta (see page 176)
4 calves' liver escalopes, about 160g each
4 tbsp olive oil, plus extra to serve
1 tbsp balsamic vinegar
1 tbsp rosemary leaves
plain flour, for rolling the polenta
vegetable oil, for rolling the polenta
celery salt and freshly ground
*   black pepper*
6 tbsp Green Tomato Chutney
*   (see page 229), to serve*

If your firm polenta has not already been prepared, you will need to start by making this following the recipe on page 176.

Preheat the oven grill to hot. Season the liver with celery salt and pepper then toss in the olive oil and vinegar. Sprinkle with the rosemary and leave to marinate for 15 minutes.

While the liver is marinating, prepare the polenta. Heat a cast-iron griddle until hot. Cut the polenta into fingers, about 6–8cm long, and roll in flour. Tap to remove any excess, then roll in vegetable oil. Place the polenta in the griddle pan and cook until lightly charred with grill lines, turning it to making a cross pattern.

Meanwhile, place the liver under the grill and grill until medium-rare – it will only take about 1–2 minutes on each side.

To serve, heat the green tomato chutney with a little olive oil and serve alongside the liver and polenta wedges.

VEGETABLE COUSCOUS
WITH DUKKAH

This dish is an all-season pleaser. In autumn and winter, the root vegetables in the hot sauce with the depth of the spices can only bring warmth and comfort. The spring and summer version makes the best of the colourful young vegetables, bringing them together in glorious harmony with the light spicing.

My mother did not know much about spicing; pepper and saffron were her staple spices and she used them only occasionally. This didn't stop her being quite adventurous. She used to buy vegetable tagine prepared to a traditional recipe from a Moroccan man at the local market. Thinking it was too spicy for us, she would add various vegetables from the garden with a bit of her own tomato sauce to soften the spicing but retain the authentic aroma.

Serves 8

Tagine base
1 fennel bulb, trimmed and cut
*   into 2cm chunks*
2 red peppers, cut into 2cm chunks
1 yellow pepper, cut into 2cm chunks
2 aubergines, cut into 2cm chunks
200g dried apricots
5 garlic cloves, finely chopped
1 fresh red chilli, deseeded
1 cinnamon stick
2 tbsp ras el hanout
grated zest of 1 lemon
1 tbsp oregano leaves
1 fresh bay leaf or 2 dried bay leaves
100ml olive oil
400g onions, finely chopped
1 x 400g can good-quality chopped
*   tomatoes*
salt and black pepper
Fast, Lightly Spiced Couscous
*   (see page 166), to serve*
green harissa, to serve

Autumn/winter
800g Jerusalem artichokes, peeled
*   and cut into 2cm chunks*
650g parsnips, peeled and cut
*   into 2cm chunks*
650g sweet potatoes, peeled and
*   cut into 2cm chunks*
450g pumpkin, peeled and
*   cut into 2cm chunks*

Spring/summer
500g broad beans, shelled
500g runner beans, topped and tailed
32 breakfast radishes
32 cherry tomatoes
500g fresh peas, shelled

Garnish
2 tbsp mint leaves
2 tbsp coriander leaves
3 tbsp flat-leaf parsley leaves
4 tbsp almond flakes, toasted

BRUNO'S TIPS

This dish would work well as an accompaniment to grilled Merguez sausages or chicken.

Preheat the oven to 200°C/fan 180°C/Gas 6. In a large roasting tin, put all the vegetables, herbs and spices except the onions. Add the autumn/winter vegetables, if using. Pour half the olive oil over the vegetables and add seasoning; mix well to make sure they are all coated with the oil. Put the tray in the oven for 10 minutes, mixing twice during that time.

Meanwhile, heat the remaining oil in a casserole or tagine. Add the chopped onions and cook over a low heat until they are soft and lightly coloured. Add the tomatoes and the roasted vegetables. Cover with 4cm of water and bring to a simmer. Skim the top then lower the heat to a very gentle simmer. Cook for about 30 minutes, until the vegetables are soft and you have a loose sauce.

If you are using the spring/summer vegetables then add them (except the peas) at this stage and cook for another 10 minutes, then add the peas and cook for a further 5 minutes.

Sprinkle with the garnish and serve with the couscous and green harissa.

CHICORY & HAM ROLLS
LIME PICKLE & YOGHURT AUBERGINES
CELERIAC & PRUNE DAUPHINOISE
POMMES SALADAISES
SPRING & SUMMER VEGETABLES
PROVENCAL TIAN
POMMES FONDANT
CRUSHED ROOT VEGETABLES WITH DUCK FAT
FAST, LIGHTLY SPICED COUSCOUS
CRUSHED PUMPKIN
BRAISED RED CABBAGE

BRAISED LENTILS
BRAISED CELERY
ROOT VEGETABLES
BAKED IN HAY
BROAD BEANS
WITH CELERY, BACON & MINT
PICKLED CABBAGE
FIRM POLENTA
CEPES A LA BORDELAISE

SIDE DISHES

CHICORY & HAM ROLLS
WITH GRATINEED COMTE CHEESE

Children are usually averse to bitter flavours and when my mother cooked this dish, even the generous layers of melting cheese on the top were not convincing enough for her children. Discussing the matter with a lady neighbour of North African origin, however, she was given the tip of adding some sugar and vinegar to the chicory during their cooking. She tried it, it was a success and this dish is now a family favourite. I add orange juice to the recipe to give it a fruity note.

Serves 4

4 chicory heads (Belgian endive)
30g butter
300ml orange juice
1 garlic clove
½ tsp thyme leaves
1 tsp sugar
2 tbsp cider vinegar
80ml double cream
2 tsp Dijon mustard
4 thin slices of Bayonne or Parma ham
100g Comté or Gruyère cheese, grated
salt and black pepper

Preheat the oven to 200°C/fan 180°C/Gas 6.

With a small knife blade, cut out the inside of the base of the chicory to make a hollow without cutting the leaves on the outside.

Melt the butter in a large frying pan over a medium heat, then add the chicory. Season with salt and pepper, then turn them to get an even golden brown colour all over.

Add the orange juice, garlic, thyme, sugar and vinegar. Bring to the boil then cover with a lid and simmer for 15 minutes or until the chicory are tender.

Remove the lid, add the cream and mustard and bring to the boil to reduce the liquid by half.

Meanwhile, lay the ham slices on a work surface, sprinkle over some cheese, then place a chicory head on top of each slice and roll up tightly. Transfer the chicory to a gratin dish.

Pour the cream mixture over, then sprinkle the top with the remaining cheese and place in the oven. Bake for about 15–20 minutes, until lightly browned on top.

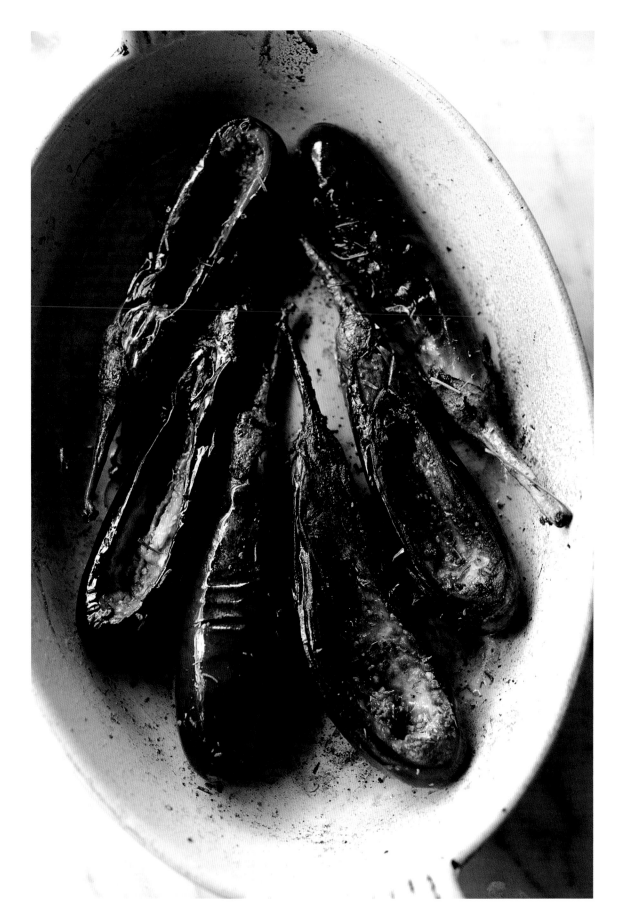

LIME PICKLE & YOGHURT AUBERGINES
WITH TOASTED ALMONDS

This dish is of course inspired by Indian cuisine. From time to time I do enjoy an Indian takeaway – in England who would not? I've long had a passion for spices and have to restrain myself at the Bistrot not to overdo it with them. Young French chefs coming to my kitchen are always taken aback by dishes like this one; they are definitely not used to these kinds of flavours in France but they usually quickly learn to appreciate them. I love this side dish with grilled oily fish, roast lamb and even with a roast chicken.

Serves 4

5 tbsp olive oil
1 onion, chopped
3 garlic cloves, chopped
1 tbsp lime pickle
½ tsp tomato purée
1 tsp onion (nigella) seeds
2 aubergines, cut into
    quarters lengthways
juice of ¼ lime
1 tbsp chopped coriander
1 tbsp flaked almonds, toasted
2 tbsp natural yoghurt
salt and black pepper

Heat 2 tablespoons of the olive oil in a frying pan over a medium heat, add the onion and the garlic. Season and cook until golden brown. Add the lime pickle, tomato purée, onion seeds and half a glass of water. Cover with a lid and leave to stew gently for about 15 minutes.

Meanwhile, heat a cast-iron griddle or barbecue until hot. Brush the quartered aubergines with the remaining olive oil, season and cook on the griddle or barbecue until soft. Cut each quarter into three pieces and add to the stewed onions. Mix well and leave to cook for a further 5 minutes.

Just before serving, add the fresh lime juice, coriander and almonds, then stir in the yoghurt and serve.

BRUNO'S TIPS

The reason I grill the aubergines instead of sautéeing them is because cooked this way they don't absorb too much oil, making the dish more digestible.

• • •

I find the lime pickle is more 'palate friendly' if I purée it in a food processor with half its volume of water, then put it back in the fridge. This dilutes it and makes the flavour less sharp. It's great mixed with olive oil and served over barbecued mackerel.

CELERIAC & PRUNE DAUPHINOISE

Gratin dauphinoise, traditionally made with potatoes, is a well–known classic. Many years ago I tried making different versions of it using root vegetables. Turnips did work well but for me celeriac had the edge. To get the same creamy texture as you would with potatoes, you will need some potato starch content, but it only needs a little. This is a fantastic side dish with game.

Serves 6

1kg celeriac, peeled and cut into quarters
150ml double cream
300ml milk, plus a little extra
    for mixing
3 garlic cloves, finely chopped
1 tsp potato starch (see Bruno's Tips)
1 tbsp chopped tarragon
⅓ tsp grated nutmeg
about 30g soft butter, for greasing
200g stoned prunes, soaked in hot water
    for 1 hour
salt and black pepper

Preheat the oven to 220°C/fan 200°C/ Gas 7. Finely slice the celeriac quarters into 3–4mm slices with a very sharp knife or, ideally, a mandoline. Place in a large mixing bowl and add the cream, milk and garlic.

In a small bowl mix the potato starch with a bit of cold milk using a whisk then pour into the larger bowl with the celeriac. Add the tarragon and season with salt, pepper and the nutmeg.

Generously butter a gratin dish. Drain the prunes and cut each into three or four pieces. Place the celeriac slices in the gratin dish arranging them by overlapping each other. Sprinkle over a few prune pieces. Build up layers of celeriac, sprinkling over some of the prunes between each layer.

Pour over the cream mixture, then bake for about 1 hour or until the celeriac is completely soft (test it with a thin knife blade) and the top is well browned.

BRUNO'S TIPS

If you have difficulty finding potato starch, use cornflour instead.

POMMES SALADAISES WITH TOMME DE SAVOIE CHEESE

Sarlat is a town in the south west of France where duck is king and truffles his queen! My mother used to cook not only potatoes but also other vegetables in duck fat. It is delicious and healthier than butter. I always have duck fat in the fridge at home and often make this dish, which is a favourite of my daughters'.

Serves 4

4 large potatoes
5 tbsp duck fat
2 garlic cloves, finely chopped
2 tbsp chopped flat-leaf parsley
60g Tomme de Savoie cheese,
    finely grated
salt and black pepper

Slice the potatoes about 3–4mm thick, ideally using a mandoline, then rinse quickly with cold water (see Bruno's Tips) and pat dry. Place the potatoes in a mixing bowl, add half the duck fat and mix well.

Heat the remaining fat in a frying pan over a medium heat. When the fat is hot, add the sliced potatoes, spreading them around. Cook to get some colour on one side, then, with a spatula, turn them over to colour the other side.

After about 15 minutes, when all the potatoes are soft and coloured and some of them crispy, add the garlic, parsley, cheese and some seasoning. Sauté well to mix it all together, then serve.

BRUNO'S TIPS

Rinsing the potatoes will rid them of excess starch and prevent them colouring too quickly.

• • •

The addition of Tomme de Savoie cheese is not a classic and can be substituted for Gruyère if you prefer, but I particularly like its flavour – it has an earthiness, which gives the dish a very rustic, hearty quality.

• • •

The dish can be left to cool, then reheated in a low oven (140°C/ fan 120°C/Gas 1) for 15–20 minutes. Personally I like to have it as a main dish for dinner with a large bowl of salad.

COCOTTE OF SPRING & SUMMER VEGETABLES

My father used to love his garden (as do I); it was his pride and joy. In spring and summer, he often used to bring home a large basket with a colourful selection of young vegetables. The look on his face and his body language sent a clear message; here was a man that was excited, proud and happy with the fruits of his labour. He always handed the basket to my mother like a beautiful bouquet of flowers. A couple of hours later, the little gems would end up in the middle of the kitchen table in a large Le Creuset cocotte, exuding the most lovely scent and confirming their organic credentials.

Serves 6

4 tbsp olive oil
12 baby carrots
6 baby fennel bulbs, trimmed and peeled
18 small radishes, trimmed
1 garlic clove
1 tbsp summer savoury
6 baby leeks, trimmed
4 runner beans, topped, tailed and
    cut into pieces
6 baby courgettes
150g podded fresh broad beans or frozen
    broad beans
150g peas
12 cherry tomatoes
6 asparagus spears
2 tbsp double cream
knob of butter
½ tsp thyme leaves
1 tbsp chopped flat-leaf parsley
2 tbsp chopped chives
1 tbsp chopped chervil
2 tbsp basil
salt and black pepper
¼ lemon, to finish

Heat the olive oil in a large pot, such as a cocotte, over a medium heat. Add the carrots, fennel and radishes. Season with salt and pepper then add the garlic and summer savoury. Stir well, cover with a lid and lower the heat as far as it will go. Cook for about 5 minutes or until the carrots are *al dente*, then remove the lid and add the baby leeks and runner beans. Stir well then add half a glass of water. Replace the lid, keeping it slightly ajar at one side. Leave to cook for 3 minutes, then add the remaining vegetables.

Mix well, then add another half-glass of water and replace the lid, again slightly ajar, and cook for a further 3 minutes. Remove the lid, then add the cream, butter and the herbs, swirl the pan to mix everything together (using a spoon to mix it might break up or damage the delicate vegetables), then squeeze over a little lemon juice. Swirl again then serve the pot in the middle of the table.

BRUNO'S TIPS

The dish can be finished by grating Parmesan cheese into the cooking liquid when you add the cream, and adding some shavings on top.

• • •

If you double the quantities, this dish will make a nice light main meal.

PROVENCAL TIAN

A *tian* is a simple gratin of Provençal vegetables that has only the moisture from the vegetables as a cooking liquid. This will evaporate during cooking to concentrate all the flavours of the south in one dish.

I like to grill the aubergines so they don't absorb too much oil. I also add fennel to the onion base, which is not in keeping with the classic version.

This would be a perfect accompaniment to any lamb or grilled fish dish, or serve it with some crumbled feta cheese over the top as a great vegetarian main course.

Serves 6

about 4 tbsp olive oil
700g onions, thinly sliced
300g fennel bulb, trimmed and thinly sliced crossways (against the grain)
4 garlic cloves, thinly sliced
1 tsp dried Provençal herbs
4 tbsp balsamic vinegar
1 aubergine
3 ripe tomatoes, sliced
1 large courgette, sliced
salt and black pepper

Preheat the oven to 180°C/fan 160°C/Gas 4.

Heat a large frying pan and add 4 teaspoons of the olive oil. Add the onions, fennel, garlic and half the Provençal herbs. Cover with a lid and leave the vegetables to wilt and the water to be released. Stir from time to time. After 20 minutes remove the lid and cook for about 5 minutes more, making sure they don't colour too much – they should be a light brown. Add the vinegar and mix well, then allow the liquid to evaporate completely.

Pour the onion mixture into a round gratin dish, spreading it over the base. Slice the aubergines into rounds, season with salt and set aside.

Heat a cast-iron griddle until hot. Brush the aubergines with a little of the remaining olive oil and cook on the griddle for about 2 minutes on each side, until marked with char lines. Arrange the vegetables in circles over the onion mixture, starting at the outside of the dish and working inwards, placing one slice of each on top of each other and alternating them so that you have a regular pattern of colour.

Drizzle over some olive oil. Sprinkle over the remaining dried herbs and season. Cover with foil and place in the oven for 20 minutes, then remove the foil and cook for another 5 minutes. The vegetables are cooked when a thin knife blade goes in easily.

ROSEMARY & BAY POMMES FONDANT

'Pommes fondant' is to the French what roast potatoes are to the British: a national classic. They're everybody's favourite and a must. Unfortunately a fondant seems to be seen as a 'cheffy' dish and only appears on restaurant menus. That's such a shame as it is so easy to make, is full of flavour and goes so well with many dishes.

Serves 6

6 Desiree potatoes, peeled
100g butter
1 tsp rosemary leaves
1 bay leaf
2 garlic cloves, crushed
80ml light veal or chicken stock
salt and black pepper

Preheat the oven to 200°C/fan 180°C/Gas 6. Using a small knife, trim the potatoes to get an even regular barrel shape with flat ends. Keep the trimmings to use in a soup, for example.

In a frying pan, melt the butter until foaming, then add the potatoes. Season and start cooking them on the stove to give then an even light golden colour, then tip them into an ovenproof dish, including all the butter. Add the rosemary and bay leaf, garlic and stock.

Using a spoon, baste the potatoes with the liquid, then place in the oven for 40 minutes, turning the potatoes every 10 minutes and basting them every 5 minutes to get an even colour.

When the potatoes are a nice golden brown colour all over and the blade of a small knife goes in easily, they are ready.

BRUNO'S TIPS

Making the potatoes a regular shape is important in this recipe so that the potatoes cook evenly and at the same speed. I know that many people find knife skills quite difficult but you can use a peeler to peel off layer after layer to shape the potatoes. It will take longer but it will give a good result.

CRUSHED ROOT VEGETABLES WITH DUCK FAT

On a cold winter night, crushed root vegetables and duck fat are a must-have experience. When I was a child, my mother would sometimes serve crushed vegetables with a generous amount of duck fat stirred through them for flavour. She would serve them on a plate with a poached duck egg sitting on top – it looked like a volcano. The egg would have been collected no sooner than the day before and tasted so fresh. A bit of home-made reduced red wine vinegar was drizzled over to cut through the richness and a crack of black pepper finished the dish. It was absolutely marvellous.

Serves 4

200g carrots, peeled and cut into chunks
150g parsnips, peeled and cut into chunks
150g celeriac, peeled and cut into chunks
200g Desiree potatoes, peeled and cut into chunks
150g swede, peeled and cut into chunks
4 garlic cloves
80g duck fat
salt and black pepper

Place the vegetables in a pan. Cover with water to 1cm above the level of the vegetables, season with salt and bring to the boil. Lower the heat, cover with a lid and leave to simmer for about 15–20 minutes or until the vegetables are soft (check by crushing them against the side of the pan with a fork).

Drain in a colander, then leave for 3 minutes to dry off before putting them back in the pan. Crush with a potato masher.

Add the duck fat and stir well with a wooden spoon. Check the seasoning and adjust if necessary.

FAST, LIGHTLY SPICED COUSCOUS

I love couscous and often have it in salad or as an accompaniment to fish or meat. The secret of success for a fluffy semolina is adding the water little by little at each stage. North Africans will traditionally steam it but that is more time-consuming and difficult with small quantities. This way is faster and works perfectly. There are different sizes of couscous available to buy; I suggest using the medium variety.

Serves 4

160g medium couscous
½ tsp ras el hanout
2 tbsp olive oil
finely grated zest of ¼ lemon
160ml boiling water
60g butter, melted
salt

Place the couscous in a bowl with the ras el hanout, olive oil, lemon zest and some salt. Mix well, then pour a third of the boiling water over and mix well. Pack it down with the back of a spoon. Cover tightly with cling film and leave in a warm place for 5 minutes.

Remove the cling film and using a fork or the palm of your hand, fluff up the couscous. Cover with another third of the boiling water and leave for a further 5 minutes, breaking it up again, then repeat with the final third of water. Add the melted butter and mix well, then serve.

CRUSHED PUMPKIN

This recipe was given to me by my friend Ramma. I believe it was passed to her by her mother, who is also a fantastic cook. The pumpkins are the perfect accompaniment to the Spicy Chicken Livers on page 106.

Serves 4

Crushed pumpkin

4 tbsp olive oil, plus extra for drizzling
1 small onion, finely chopped
1 tsp chopped curry leaves
1 tsp black mustard seeds
1 tsp cumin seeds
4 garlic cloves
1 red chilli, chopped
600g pumpkin, peeled, deseeded and diced
1 tbsp lemon juice
½ tsp caster sugar (optional; see Bruno's Tips)
salt and black pepper

Garnish

pomegranate seeds, to taste
chopped flat-leaf parsley

Heat the oil in a large non-stick frying pan over a medium–high heat. Add the onion and sauté until translucent. Add the curry leaves, mustard and cumin seeds and fry for 1 minute. Crush the garlic with the chilli to make a paste, then add this to the mixture, stirring quickly for a few seconds (the onion will start to turn slightly golden). Add the pumpkin, season with salt and pepper and mix well. Reduce the heat slightly and cook, covered, for 15–20 minutes, stirring every couple of minutes until the pumpkin has collapsed and turned mushy. Add the lemon juice and sugar, if using (if you have quite a sweet pumpkin you may not need sugar so taste the pumpkin before you add it), then continue to cook for a further 5 minutes to caramelise the pumpkin, stirring constantly. Depending on personal preference, you can either mash the pumpkin or just crush it. Sometimes, if the pumpkin is not juicy enough, it may need a bit of water to help it soften and mash. Drizzle over a little more olive oil, and sprinkle over the pomegranate seeds and parsley before serving.

BRUNO'S TIPS

You can use honey or any form of sweetener instead of sugar.

BRAISED RED CABBAGE & RED BERRIES

Red cabbage is not very fashionable and is, in my opinion, underused. Sliced very finely, it needs only a balsamic dressing and orange segments to make a delicious winter salad. Or why not add it to coleslaw? But in the recipe below, I braise it with red fruits and vinegar, giving it a great balance of sweet, sour and fruity. It's a must with a game casserole, and generally great with any red meat in winter. In the UK, red berries are of course a summer fruit so I've used frozen berries in this recipe, which work just as well.

Serves 4

50g butter
2 Cox's apples, peeled, cored and diced
⅓ tsp caraway seeds
½ bay leaf
½ red cabbage, finely sliced
1 onion, finely sliced
2 tbsp redcurrant jelly
3 tbsp red wine vinegar
250g mixed red berries (defrosted
    if frozen)
salt and black pepper

Melt the butter in a pan and add the apples, caraway seeds and bay leaf. Mix well and cook over a medium heat for a couple of minutes to soften the apple a little, then add the cabbage and onion. Season and mix well, then add the redcurrant jelly and vinegar. Mix again, then reduce the heat to low, cover with a lid and cook slowly for 40 minutes, mixing from time to time.

Add the berries, mix well and cook uncovered for a further 15 minutes. Check the seasoning before serving.

BRUNO'S TIPS

This dish tastes even better the day after it's cooked as the flavours intensify, so I would suggest making it the day before you want to serve it.

MY CHILDHOOD BRAISED LENTILS

My parents were by no means wealthy but as a child I sometimes felt very privileged to eat the way we did. My mother was very busy with seven children to look after but somehow always seemed to find the time to cook a good meal. I wish she were still here so I could tell her how much use I have made of her recipes, both in my repertoire and in this book. When I serve lentils in the winter at the Bistrot I do it the way my mother used to do it. Nothing has changed as I simply don't know a better way. These lentils are particularly good with sausages or roast pork.

Serves 4

400g green puy or castelluccio lentils
½ bay leaf
1 tsp thyme leaves
20g butter
200g unsmoked pancetta, cut into
    small dice
2 onions, finely sliced
a handful of flat-leaf parsley leaves,
    roughly chopped
2 garlic cloves, chopped
2 tbsp red wine vinegar
salt and black pepper

Place the lentils in a pan. Cover with water by 5cm then bring to the boil. Lower the heat to a simmer and skim the surface. Add the bay leaf and thyme leaves. Simmer for about 20 minutes or until the lentils are tender but still hold their shape.

While the lentils are cooking, heat the butter in a frying pan. When foaming, cook the pancetta with the onions and thyme over a medium heat, stirring from time to time. When the onions are light brown and soft, pour the mixture into a food processor and add the parsley, garlic and vinegar. Process to a fine purée, then stir into the lentils. Check the seasoning. Mix well and leave to settle for 3–5 minutes before serving.

BRUNO'S TIPS

When my family and I cook this in France we use 'ventreche', a peppery dry-cured bacon instead of pancetta but sadly it is very difficult to find in the UK.

BRAISED CELERY

I love braised celery! I think this wonderful vegetable is underrated yet it is so versatile. The sticks can be thinly sliced and used in salads, soups, risottos and stews. And the heart can be cut into two or four depending on its size and, as it is here, braised, which is the perfect accompaniment to a roast. My mother used to serve it with roast veal or guinea fowl.

Serves 6

3 bunches of celery
50g butter
100g carrots, finely diced
1 small onion, finely diced
1 tbsp tarragon vinegar
6 tbsp light soy sauce
1 tsp sugar
freshly ground black pepper
roughly chopped flat-leaf parsley,
*   to garnish*

Cut the celery bunches 12cm from the base. Take off the first layer of sticks, keeping only the tender yellow ones. Cut these lengths in half.

In a frying pan, melt the butter, then add the celery and cook gently over a medium heat for about 20 minutes, until lightly coloured on both sides. Remove the celery with a slotted spoon, reduce the heat to low, then add the carrots and onion to the pan. Cook for about 5 minutes, to soften, then replace the celery, add the vinegar, soy sauce, sugar and a sprinkling of pepper and finally a glass of water. Cover with a lid and simmer gently for 20–30 minutes or until the celery is very tender.

Remove the lid and increase the heat to evaporate off most of the liquid and create a glaze. Garnish with parsley and serve.

BRUNO'S TIPS

Gem lettuces can be cooked in the same way, though they need less cooking time – about 10 minutes.

• • •

Keep the outside sticks of celery and use them for soups, salads or stews.

ROOT VEGETABLES BAKED IN HAY

I love this dish! Root vegetables, fresh out of the ground, cooked with only their own moisture and the scent of the country hay. It could not be simpler and more natural. Perhaps I am also fond of this technique because it reminds me of the way my grandfather used to cook chestnuts in the fireplace. He used to pull out some embers then lay the chestnuts over them and cover them with another thick layer of embers, adding more from time to time when they burned out. After about 1½ hours we used to savour the chestnuts, eating them around the fireplace with a glass of fermented grape juice, a local speciality called 'bourru' and a large bowl of wild dandelions. I miss that life!

Serves 6

6 purple carrots
6 baby yellow carrots
6 baby orange carrots
6 baby golden beetroots
6 Georgia beetroots
6 shallots
3 heads of garlic
6 young potatoes
6 small parsnips
2 sprigs of rosemary
4 sage leaves
sea salt and freshly ground black pepper

You will also need 4 handfuls of hay

Preheat the oven to 200°C/fan 180°C/Gas 6. Wash the hay at least three times, then drain and pat dry.

Cut the green tops off the vegetables, leaving at least 2cm at the root, then wash and brush all the vegetables.

Cut out a layer of foil big enough to hold all the vegetables, then cut another the same size and double them up. Spread half the hay over the foil then lay the vegetables on top. Season with salt and pepper. Sprinkle over the rosemary and sage then cover with the remaining hay. Close the foil tightly then place the parcel on a baking tray in the oven for about 1 hour.

To serve, place the parcel on a dish and open the foil at the table so that everyone can pick their own vegetables.

Eat this with your fingers – it's fantastic!

BRUNO'S TIPS

This recipe is delicious served as a dish in its own right with Béarnaise sauce as dip.

BROAD BEANS
WITH CELERY, BACON & MINT

When fully grown and dried, broad beans have a brown colour and are packed with proteins. My dad used to love them stewed with black pudding and a lot of garlic. We used to buy them from the local market in Libourne but we also used to grow our own in the summer and eat those very young, fresh from the pods, dipped in salt with a buttered piece of sourdough bread. Sometimes my mother would cook them as in the recipe below, not with mint but with summer savoury.

Serves 4

1.5kg fresh broad beans or 500g frozen
    broad beans in their skins
60g butter
150g smoked streaky bacon, cut into
    dice or strips
150g celery, cut into small cubes
1 onion, chopped
2 garlic cloves, chopped
a handful of mint, roughly chopped
salt and black pepper

If using fresh beans, take them out of their pods and plunge them into boiling salted water for 30 seconds, then drain and refresh in cold water. Peel off the skin to reveal the beautiful vivid green beans. If using frozen beans, remove from their skins (see Bruno's Tip).

In a saucepan, heat half the butter over a medium heat. When foaming, add the bacon, cook for 3 minutes, then add the celery, onion and garlic. Stir well with a spoon and cook for about 4 minutes until the onion is softened and very lightly coloured. Add the broad beans and a small glass of water. Bring to the boil then stir in the remaining butter and mint. Check the seasoning and serve immediately.

BRUNO'S TIPS

If you are using frozen broad beans, place the frozen beans in a bowl. Cover with hot water from the tap then leave for 2 minutes. Empty the water and replace with cold water. Squeeze the beans one by one to pop them out of their skins.

PICKLED CABBAGE

I first ate this cabbage in Hong Kong where I was doing some consultancy work for a French brasserie. In fact it was served for the staff dinner along with leftover pork, all knocked up by an apprentice chef in about 15 minutes. It has become a favourite of mine and I sometimes serve it at the Bistrot.

Serves 6

750g Chinese cabbage, cut into
    2cm squares
3 tbsp sea salt
2 tbsp soft light brown sugar
60ml peanut oil
1 onion, chopped
4 garlic cloves, chopped
2 red chillies, deseeded and chopped
30g fresh root ginger, peeled
    and chopped
1 tbsp Szechuan pepper
1 tsp English mustard
100ml brown rice vinegar
chopped coriander, to garnish

Place the cabbage in a bowl. Sprinkle with the salt and sugar and mix well with your hands, squeezing the cabbage, for 2 minutes to massage in the salt and sugar. Leave at room temperature for 2 hours, repeating the mixing every 30 minutes.

In a wok, heat the oil over a high heat, then add the onion, garlic, chilli, ginger, Szechuan pepper and mustard. Stir-fry for 10 seconds then lower the heat to medium to soften the ingredients.

Meanwhile, drain the cabbage and squeeze out any excess liquid. Add to the wok, stir, then remove from the heat. Add the vinegar. Pour all the ingredients into a glass or china dish and cover with cling film. This leaves the cabbage to relax, while also retaining its moisture. Serve warm or at room temperature.

FIRM POLENTA

Polenta is made from corn and is associated with Italy. When I was a child we used to eat it as a speciality from the Pyrenees (where my father came from) as a dish in which polenta was cooked with water, pork fat and rum then pan-fried in butter with sugar – delicious on cold winter nights.

Serves 6

500ml water
100g instant polenta
30g Parmesan cheese, grated
30g butter
1 tsp salt

Bring the water to the boil, then add the polenta in a fine stream, whisking continuously until the mixture starts to boil again. Keep whisking for another minute, then switch to a wooden spoon and stir the polenta over a low heat until it detaches itself from the sides of the pan – it should take about 15 minutes. Add the Parmesan, butter and salt. Mix well and pour into a baking tray lined with cling film to a thickness of 2cm. Cool completely and place in the fridge until ready to use.

CEPES A LA BORDELAISE

One of my hobbies is walking in the woods and, in season, picking mushrooms; I find it very relaxing. In fact I only look for ceps. In southwest France the cep is the king of mushrooms and is always revered on the table. It is usually cooked with shallots, garlic and parsley; a simple recipe that allows the flavour of the mushrooms to come through. When I was a child, my father used to take my brothers and me mushroom-picking and taught us what to look for. We used to walk for hours in the woods to find ceps. Still today, beautifully formed ceps, standing proudly like they have been carved out of butter, is one of the best and most rewarding sights. However, I would discourage anyone who has not been trained from picking mushrooms. You need to know exactly what you are doing otherwise it can be dangerous. The ceps in this recipe can be replaced by chestnut mushrooms and/or wild mushrooms, which are readily available when in season.

Serves 4

800g fresh ceps
2 tbsp duck fat
3 tbsp finely chopped shallots
1 garlic clove, finely chopped
2 tbsp chopped flat-leaf parsley
salt and black pepper

With a small knife, lightly trim the bottom of the cep stalks, removing all the earth. Fill a bowl with cold water, then lightly dip the ceps into it one by one, cleaning them delicately with a brush. The idea is to let them have minimum contact with the water so that they don't get soggy and don't lose their flavour. Pat dry thoroughly, then cut into chunky pieces.

In a frying pan, heat 1 tablespoon of the duck fat until fairly hot then add half the ceps, stir to colour them on all sides, then remove to a plate. Add the remaining duck fat and repeat with the remaining ceps, then remove them with a slotted spoon.

In the same pan, cook the shallots and garlic over a medium heat until they soften and colour lightly. Return the ceps to the pan and add the parsley.

Season with salt and pepper, toss well for a minute and serve immediately.

TARTE AU SUCRE
PRUNE & ARMAGNAC
STICKY PUDDING
RIZ A L'IMPERATRICE
CREPES SUZETTE
RHUBARB
CLERKENWELL MESS
FRENCH TOAST TERRINE WITH
TARRAGON-POACHED PEARS
PEACH & BURNT BUTTER TART
GRAND MARNIER ECLAIRS
FRESH RASPBERRIES
WITH SOFT LEMON
TARTE AUX POMMES
CHILLI & GINGER
ROASTED PINEAPPLE
CHOCOLATE &
ORANGE SOUFFLE

GOATS' MILK PANNA COTTA,
WITH CANDIED TOMATOES
LIGHT CHRISTMAS PIE
SALTED CARAMEL
& COCONUT MACAROONS
KAFFIR LIME ICED PARFAIT
WITH LIQUORICE FIGS
STRAWBERRIES
ON ELDERFLOWER JELLY,
& CHAMPAGNE
STRAWBERRY
& BALSAMIC JAM
FRESH RASPBERRY MOUSSE
WITH BASIL SYRUP

PUDDINGS

TARTE AU SUCRE

Perouges is a stunningly beautiful little medieval walled village 30km from Lyon. It is postcard-perfect. Perouges is also famous for its *tarte au sucre*, a sugar- and cream-topped kind of brioche tart. The sweet buttery and yeasty smell makes this an irresistible afternoon treat with a cup of coffee.

Serves 6–8

5g fast-action dried yeast
175ml lukewarm water
1 tbsp caster sugar
350g plain flour, plus extra for dusting
2 eggs, plus 1 egg yolk
a pinch of salt
160g butter, softened and cut into cubes

Topping
70g crème fraîche
60g caster sugar
60g demerara sugar
grated zest of 1 lemon

In a mixing bowl, dissolve the yeast in the water, then add the sugar and 50g of the flour. Whisk well to avoid lumps, then cover with cling film and place in a warm place for about 15 minutes – the mixture should become bubbly and double in volume.

Place the remaining flour in the bowl of an electric mixer fitted with the dough hook. Add the eggs, egg yolk, salt and the yeast and mix on a medium speed. It will take about 5 minutes for the dough to get some elasticity; then you can add the butter. Add it in small amounts – just a few cubes at a time – making sure it is fully incorporated before adding the next bit. Once all the butter is added mix for another 2 minutes, until the dough is elastic.

Place the dough in a lightly floured bowl, cover with a damp cloth and place in the fridge for an hour.

Preheat the oven to 195°C/fan 175°C/ Gas 5½.

Form the dough into a ball and place on a lightly floured work surface. Roll out to a 32–35cm diameter circle. Carefully transfer to a baking sheet (I use a non-stick pizza tray), then, with the tip of a finger, push the dough about 1cm in from the edge all around to form a small rim/border.

For the topping, spread the crème fraîche all over the tart using the back of a spoon, then sprinkle over the sugars and lemon zest and bake for about 20 minutes, until it feels spongy and is golden brown all over. Make sure to check the underneath is cooked, too.

BRUNO'S TIPS

If you like you can bake the tart with some poached fruit spread over the sugar topping. Apricots or cherries work well in summer; rhubarb in winter, or simply serve it with a good home-made jam.

PRUNE & ARMAGNAC STICKY PUDDING

Prune and Armagnac is a classic pairing of flavours from the south west of France. It has been made famous in England along with dishes such as pistachio soufflé, *pied de cochon farçi* and others by the legendary Pierre Koffmann at La Tante Claire restaurant in Chelsea. The flavours work really well in this pudding and are a nice alternative to the sticky toffee pudding usually made with dates. My mother used to make prunes in syrup and Armagnac and store them in jars in the cellar. They were a treat on Sunday afternoons to have with family and friends!

Serves 6

300g prunes, stoned (150g chopped;
    150g puréed in a blender)
1 tsp bicarbonate of soda
300ml hot water
100g very soft butter, plus extra
    to grease
170g dark brown sugar
2 eggs
170g self-raising flour
1 tsp vanilla essence
1 tsp finely grated orange zest
Armagnac, to finish
250ml crème fraîche, to serve

Sauce
200g dark brown sugar
200g double cream
80g butter
80g dark treacle

Preheat the oven to 200°C/fan 180°C/Gas 6. Butter 6 holes of a large muffin tin.

In a bowl mix the chopped prunes and prune purée with the bicarbonate of soda, then pour over the hot water. Stir and keep aside.

In another mixing bowl, beat the butter and sugar until pale, then add the eggs one at a time, whisking continuously. Fold in a tablespoon of flour with the final egg to prevent curdling. Gently fold in the remaining flour, then stir in the prune mixture with the vanilla and orange zest. Pour the mixture into the tin then bake for 20 minutes or until a fine blade or skewer inserted into the centre of a pudding comes out dry.

Meanwhile, bring all the ingredients for the sauce to the boil in a small pan, then lower the heat and simmer for 5 minutes.

Take the puddings out of the tin and pour 2 tablespoons of the sauce into each mould. Put the puddings back in the moulds and place in the oven for 2 minutes.

Just before serving, splash a bit of Armagnac onto each pudding, then turn out. Place the puddings on plates and serve with the crème fraîche, or pouring cream if you prefer.

BRUNO'S TIPS

You can use an electric mixer to mix the ingredients more easily.

• • •

If you don't have Armagnac, use a good dark rum.

RIZ A L'IMPERATRICE

This rice pudding is an old French classic; I learned it over 35 years ago at catering school in Bordeaux, as it was part of the curriculum. Over the years I've made very few changes to the basic recipe but I've played with the flavouring components and have changed the type of rice. This is a comfort-food pudding with an elegant look to it. It's definitely a crowd pleaser and my kind of dessert.

Serves 6

500ml milk
1 vanilla pod, split in half
½ tsp grated orange zest
40g golden raisins
80g caster sugar
100g sushi rice
80g glacé cherries, diced
30g angelica
250ml double cream
3 tbsp kirsch

Crème anglaise
4 egg yolks
60g caster sugar
375ml milk
2 gelatine leaves, soaked in
    water until soft

Garnish
200g redcurrant jelly
1 gelatine leaf, soaked in
    water until soft
9 poached apricots, halved

First, make the crème anglaise. Place the egg yolks and sugar in a mixing bowl and whisk until the sugar dissolves and the mixture turns pale white.

Bring the milk to the boil, then remove from the heat and pour it over the egg mixture, whisking well. Pour the mixture back into the pan, and place over a very low heat. Stir continuously until the mixture is thick enough to coat the back of a spoon, then remove from the heat and pour it into a clean bowl. Squeeze the gelatine to remove any water, then add to the bowl and stir well. Place the bowl into another bowl of iced water to cool completely.

To cook the rice, place the milk and vanilla pod in a pan and bring to the boil. Add the orange zest, raisins and sugar, then add the rice and stir well. Cover the surface of the liquid with a circle of greaseproof paper then a lid and cook over a low heat for about 30 minutes or until the rice is cooked.

When the rice is cooked, remove the vanilla pod, add the glacé cherries and the angelica, then pour the mixture into a large bowl set in another of iced water. Leave to cool completely, stirring from time to time. When completely cold and the mixture is

starting to set around the sides, mix in the crème anglaise.

Whisk the cream in a mixing bowl until thick, stir in the kirsch, then fold into the rice. Pour the rice into serving glasses – martini glasses are ideal – or I like to use rectangular moulds or rings (oiled with a spray). Place in the fridge for about 30 minutes, until set.

When the puddings are almost set, heat the redcurrant jelly in a small pan with 2 tablespoons of water. Squeeze the gelatine to remove any water, then add it to the pan. Remove the pan from the heat and mix well with a spoon. Cool a little then pour the mixture over and around the rice puddings. Transfer to the fridge to set.

If using the rectangles or rings, lightly heat the sides with a blow torch or wrap a hot damp tea towel around them, unmould the pudding on to the middle of the plate, then arrange the apricots, overlapping them, on the top. If using the glasses, simply lay the apricots on top.

BRUNO'S TIPS

In season, peaches or raspberries could replace the apricots.

CREPES SUZETTE
WITH A TOUCH OF CARDAMOM

Flour, milk and eggs are the three main ingredients needed to make lovely French crêpes. Yes, it is that simple! Writing this recipe takes me down memory lane and reminds me of the respect my parents had for what appear to be quite basic products today. I often lecture my chefs at the Bistrot on how respectful they have to be towards food and often quote the following family story.

For my parents, the restrictions during and after the war left big scars. The French social troubles of May 1968 reminded them that nothing should be taken for granted. My mother used to encourage my brothers and me to hide bags of flour and sugar in the bedroom ceilings or jars of preserves under the coal in the cellar. She used to tell us that it was a secret and we could not tell anyone; it was just in case.

Serves 4 (makes about 8 pancakes)

50g sugar
2 tbsp lemon juice
150ml fresh orange juice (without 'bits')
2 cardamom pods, finely crushed
finely grated zest of ¼ orange
50g butter
4 tbsp Grand Marnier
2 oranges, peeled and segmented

Crêpes
125g plain flour
a pinch of salt
2 tbsp sugar
2 eggs
200ml milk
50ml lager
1 tbsp vanilla extract
25g butter
vegetable oil, for frying

Start by making the crêpe batter. Place the flour, salt and sugar in a mixing bowl and make a well in the centre. Break the eggs into a small bowl and mix with the milk, lager and vanilla until thoroughly combined.

Start to pour the egg mixture into the well in the flour in a fine stream, bringing the flour into the liquid little by little and whisking to incorporate it. Stop pouring the liquid when the mixture is still quite thick, similar to a mayonnaise consistency. At this point, if the mixture has any lumps, a good whisk should eliminate them. Pour the remaining egg mixture in, whisking continuously.

In a small pan, melt the butter and cook it over a medium heat until it turns a nutty brown colour (a 'beurre noisette'), then remove from the heat and pour it into the crêpe mixture. Whisk well. Leave the mixture to rest at room temperature for 30 minutes.

Stir the crêpe batter well. Spread a thin layer of vegetable oil over the base of a large crêpe pan or frying pan, then place it over a medium heat until hot. Pour a large spoonful of batter into the pan, swirling the pan to spread the mixture as evenly as possible. The trick is to have just enough to cover the pan.

Reduce the heat to medium–low. Be careful, the crêpe will be coloured enough in about 30 seconds, so flip it over to cook the other side for another 30 seconds. Remove from the pan and place it on a cool kitchen surface for 2 minutes, then repeat. Pile the crêpes on a plate, covering them with a clean damp tea towel.

Once the crêpes are all cooked, use the same frying pan to heat the sugar to start to make a light-coloured caramel then add the lemon and orange juices with the crushed cardamom and orange zest. Bring to the boil, then add the butter and Grand Marnier. Flambé the alcohol using a match, then turn the heat down to low.

Fold the crêpes in half then roll each one up to make a cone shape. Place four crêpes in the pan at a time and heat them through, turning to coat them in the mixture. Add the orange segments and turn them over in the mixture, too. Transfer to a hot plate and cover tightly with cling film.

To serve, place two pancakes on each serving plate then spoon over the hot sauce and orange segments.

BRUNO'S TIPS

Serve with a vanilla or passion fruit ice cream, if you can find it.

• • •

I also like crêpes served plain with pears, peeled and sliced, then pan-fried in butter. You make a caramel sauce by heating 60g of sugar in the same way as above, then stirring in 60ml double cream. You then add the pears and serve over plain crêpes.

RHUBARB CLERKENWELL MESS

Most people have heard of Eton Mess: beautifully perfumed strawberries, mixed with crunchy sweet meringue and cream. It's a classic English summer pudding and I love its homely feel.

English rhubarb is at its best between mid-January and May and it must be used. After a long period of making crumbles I felt like a change and came up with this fun interpretation of the original Eton version, which I have called Clerkenwell Mess due to the location of the Bistrot. It generates curiosity and now it outsells the crumble.

Serves 4

500g pink rhubarb, cut into 6cm pieces
150g caster sugar
100ml orange juice
½ tsp finely chopped fresh root ginger
1 gelatine leaf, soaked in cold water
    until soft then squeezed of
    excess water
50ml elderflower cordial
150ml whipping cream
1 tsp vanilla extract
4 meringues, about 6cm wide, crushed
1 large pink grapefruit, peeled
    and segmented
icing sugar, to dust

Preheat the oven to 220°C/fan 200°C/ Gas 7. Set aside four pieces of the rhubarb, then place the remainder in a bowl with the sugar, orange juice and ginger. Transfer to a small pan and bring to the boil. Skim the surface with a spoon, then cover with a lid, reduce the heat to low and cook for 5 minutes, until the rhubarb is tender. Remove from the heat and pour into a colander set over a clean bowl to cool. Add the gelatine to the cooking liquid then transfer to the fridge for 1 hour to set.

Once the oven is hot, turn it off. Slice the four reserved pieces of rhubarb very finely (ideally using a mandoline). Line a baking sheet with cling film and dust with icing sugar. Bring the cordial to the boil, remove from the heat and add the sliced rhubarb. Leave it for 30 seconds then gently lift out the rhubarb and place it on a clean tea towel. Transfer the

rhubarb to the prepared baking sheet, laying it side by side, then dust over more icing sugar. Place in the oven (turned off) overnight to crisp up. Alternatively you can bake them in the oven for 30 minutes at 100°C/ fan 80°C/Gas ¼.

Whip the cream with the vanilla until soft peaks form. Fill four individual glass serving dishes with equal amounts of the cream, meringue, rhubarb, jelly and pink grapefruit segments. Stir roughly to create a 'mess'. Decorate the top with the rhubarb crisps.

BRUNO'S TIPS

You could create your own 'mess' by using other fruits of your choice.

FRENCH TOAST TERRINE WITH TARRAGON-POACHED PEARS

French toast or 'pain perdu' (lost bread) was always one of my favourite snacks when I came home from school in the afternoons. The problem was that we only had it on rare occasions because 'pain perdu' is traditionally made with stale bread, which we didn't usually have in our house. The version below is a more 'cheffy' one for a dinner party with guests but you could keep it simpler by pan-frying the bread and missing out the terrine stage. I would suggest you keep the tarragon pears, though, as they are truly amazing.

Serves 8

600ml whole milk
60g caster sugar
2 eggs, plus 4 egg yolks
1 vanilla pod, split in half and
    seeds scraped
8 thick slices of stale bread
80g butter
a dollop of crème fraîche, to serve

Poached pears
8 ripe pears, such as Williams, peeled
    (reserve the peelings)
500g jam sugar (with pectin)
1 litre water
50ml tarragon vinegar
50 fresh tarragon leaves

BRUNO'S TIPS

I would suggest that you prepare this recipe the day before so the pears can marinate in their poaching liquid and absorb all the flavours. The terrine will also benefit from a longer rest as it will hold better when slicing.

For the poached pears, place the pear peelings, sugar and water in a small pan. Bring to the boil and boil for 2 minutes, then add the vinegar, tarragon leaves and pears. Bring to a simmer, then lower the heat to a very gentle simmer, and cover the surface with greaseproof paper. Make a hole in the middle for the steam to escape. The cooking time will vary, depending on the pears you use, but if they are ripe and soft, check the cooking after 10 minutes: a thin knife blade should go through the flesh easily. Leave the pears to cool in their liquid. Once cool, transfer to the fridge.

Put the milk, sugar, eggs, egg yolks and vanilla seeds in a mixing bowl. (Reserve the empty vanilla pod and place it in a jar with caster sugar to make vanilla sugar.) Using a hand blender, blitz the mix well.

Soak each slice of bread in the mixture for a few minutes. Heat some of the butter in a frying pan until foaming, then pan-fry the bread until golden brown on each side. Repeat, adding more butter between batches, until all the slices are cooked.

Preheat the oven to 200°C/fan 180°C/ Gas 6. Line a 22 x 6cm tin or terrine mould with a piece of foil. Put a bit of the soaking mixture into the bottom of the mould. Add a layer of the sliced bread, filling any gaps by cutting up one of the other slices of bread. Add another thin layer of mixture, then another layer of bread. Repeat until all the bread and mixture has been used.

Bake for 20 minutes then place the tin on a wire rack to cool. When cool, transfer to the fridge to chill completely (see Bruno's Tip).

Meanwhile, lift the pears out of their poaching syrup and transfer to a plate, then return to the fridge. Pass half the pear poaching liquid through a fine sieve into a small pan and place over a medium heat to bubble and reduce to a third of its original volume – it should be syrupy. Chill this syrup.

When the terrine is cold, turn out on to a plate and cut into eight slices. Place a slice in the middle of a serving plate and top with a pear. Divide the syrup among the plates and serve with a dollop of crème fraîche.

PEACH & BURNT BUTTER TART

When my mother made a dessert, it was often a tart. They are a simple one-job wonder and her large tart tin was just big enough to be able to cut slices for the nine of us around the table.

The pastry I've used here is an unsweetened 'pâte brisée' (shortcrust pastry), which I use in preference to a sweet dough as it is crispy and buttery. Using a plain dough also adds a nice contrast to the sweet filling.

My mother simply added melted butter to her tart filling but I've amended that by browning it to improve the butter's flavour; a technique that I've found works well in many dishes.

Serves 6–8

1 egg, plus 2 egg yolks
50g caster sugar
1 vanilla pod, split in half, seeds scraped
200ml double cream
50g butter
60g ground almonds
2 drops of almond essence
12 poached peaches (see Bruno's Tips), halved
icing sugar, to dust
6 tbsp crème fraiche, to serve

Shortcrust pastry
180g butter, cut into small dice
240g plain flour, plus extra to dust
a pinch of salt
1 tsp finely grated lemon zest
60ml water

For the pastry, spread the diced butter out on a plate. Place the flour on a work surface then make a well in the middle and sprinkle over the salt.

Put the lemon zest in a small bowl and add 3 tablespoons of flour from the well. Mix with the lemon, then dust over the well. Place the butter in the well, then bring the flour into the centre and with the tips of your fingers work it all together so that it resembles coarse breadcrumbs.

Make another well in the centre then add the water. Mix quickly then knead it for a few moments, just until it comes together. The dough will be quite lumpy. Make a ball with the dough, then flatten it a bit. Wrap in cling film and chill for 30 minutes.

Preheat the oven to 220°C/fan 200°C/Gas 7. Lightly grease a 23cm tart tin. Lightly flour a work surface and roll out the pastry. The diameter of the pastry should be 5cm larger than the tart tin. Check the size by turning the tart tin upside down on top of the pastry. Roll the pastry gently on to the rolling pin then unroll it over the tin.

Push the pastry into the edges of the tin, pressing against the sides with your thumbs. Let the pastry hang over the edge of the tin, then cut off the overhang leaving just 1cm.

Place in the freezer for 10 minutes, then cover with greaseproof paper and fill the inside with baking beans or dried beans. Bake for 15 minutes, then remove the beans and paper and bake for a further 5 minutes, until golden and crisp.

Remove from the oven and set aside. Reduce the oven setting to 195°C/fan 175°C/Gas 5½.

Meanwhile, make the filling. Place the eggs, egg yolks, sugar and the vanilla seeds in a mixing bowl. Whisk well, until pale and creamy, then pour the cream over.

Heat the butter in a frying pan until foaming and turning light brown, then quickly pour it into the egg mixture, whisking well. Stir in the ground almonds and almond essence. Mix again.

Pour a quarter of the mixture into the pastry case then arrange six peach halves around the outside edge of the tart, then cut the other six halves in half again and arrange them in the middle.

Pour the remaining mixture into the case then bake in the oven for 25–30 minutes, until golden brown on top.

Leave the tart to rest for at least 5 minutes before serving as it will cut more cleanly. Dust with icing sugar and serve with crème fraîche.

BRUNO'S TIPS

You can buy ready-made poached peaches but you can also poach them yourself. Bring 1 litre of water mixed with 500g sugar to the boil, then add the juice of 1 lemon and simmer for 3 minutes, then add the whole peaches and poach until tender.

• • •

After blind baking the pastry, brush the inside of the shell with an egg yolk and place in the oven for 30 seconds before filling. This will create an impermeable barrier and the pastry will be more crispy.

• • •

For an even better presentation, glaze the tart by brushing it with warmed apricot jam.

GRAND MARNIER ECLAIRS

I know they don't feel like a dessert – more like a pastry to be enjoyed with afternoon tea – but I love éclairs. As a child I used to save up and buy one or two at the local pastry shop, then sit at the back of the nearby church and 'religiously' savour the forbidden delights, not having to share them with anyone. I remember when I was 14 I had my first attempt at re-creating this beautiful pastry. The result was so good that my mother never believed I had made the éclairs myself and questioned where I got the money to buy enough of them for a family of nine. What a fabulous way to finish a meal – eating with your hands and licking your fingers!

Serves 8

Dough
125ml milk
125ml water
80g butter
20g caster sugar
a pinch of salt
150g plain flour
3 eggs, lightly beaten

Egg wash
1 egg yolk, beaten with 2 tbsp milk

Mousseline cream
2 egg yolks
35g caster sugar
20g cornflour
200ml milk
*⅓ leaf of gelatine soaked in
    cold water until soft, then
    squeezed of excess water*
20g butter
1 tsp vanilla extract
125ml whipping cream
2 tbsp Grand Marnier

Preheat the oven to 195°C/fan 175°C/Gas 5½. To make the dough, place the milk, water, butter, sugar and salt in a saucepan and bring to the boil. As soon as it starts to boil, remove from the heat, then add the flour. Mix well with a wooden spoon, beating the mixture on the side of the pan until smooth. Return the pan to a medium heat for a couple of minutes, stirring continuously. Transfer the mix to a small mixing bowl and continue to mix while you add the egg little by little. The mix should be shiny and smooth.

Pour the mixture into a piping bag fitted with a 15mm plain nozzle. Line a baking tray with greaseproof paper and pipe the éclairs in the shape of large fingers, about 12cm long. With the back of a fork, dipped in the egg wash, create a line pattern across the fingers then brush the top with a little of the egg wash. Cook in the oven for about 25–30 minutes or until crisp on the outside.

Meanwhile, make the mousseline cream. In a mixing bowl, whisk the egg yolks and sugar until pale, then add the cornflour. Bring the milk to the boil and pour over the egg mixture, whisking continuously. Pour the mixture back into the pan then cook over a medium heat until it boils. Stir continuously and cook for another 5 minutes. Remove from the heat and add the gelatine, butter and vanilla. Mix well then place in a bowl inside a larger bowl of iced water to cool completely.

When cool, place in an electric mixer fitted with the paddle attachment. Mix well until the mix becomes pale yellow to white, then transfer to the fridge.

Meanwhile, whip the cream until the whisk leaves a ribbon trail when lifted, then add the Grand Marnier and mix well. Fold the whipped cream into the pastry cream mixture.

Make a small hole at both ends of the éclairs. Place the mousseline cream mixture in a piping bag fitted with a very small plain nozzle and fill the éclairs from one side then from the other. Alternatively you could simply slice the éclairs horizontally and fill one half, then replace the lid.

FRESH RASPBERRIES WITH SOFT LEMON MERINGUE

Red fruits in the UK are probably the best in the world and a classic dessert such as a summer pudding is one of the best tributes to them. I particularly appreciate the delicate flavour of raspberries and think that this recipe does them justice, preserving the full identity of this fruit by outlining its grace. This dish is based on an old French classic – 'île flottante' (floating island) – that my grandmother often used to make for the big family table. It was delicious and definitely the masterpiece of the meal as far as the children were concerned.

Serves 6

4 egg whites
a pinch of salt
4 tbsp caster sugar, plus extra for
*   the moulds*
½ tsp finely grated lemon zest
30g butter
500g fresh raspberries

Crème anglaise
4 egg yolks
60g caster sugar
350ml whole milk
1 tsp vanilla extract or ½ a vanilla pod,
*   split in half and seeds scraped*

Preheat the oven to 195°C/fan 175°C/ Gas 5½. Start by making the crème anglaise. In a mixing bowl, whisk the egg yolks with the sugar until the mix becomes pale.

In a small pan, bring the milk to the boil with the vanilla pod, if using, then remove from the heat and pour over the egg yolks, whisking continuously. Pour the mixture back into the pan and place over a very low heat. Stir continuously until the mixture is thick enough to coat the back of a spoon, then immediately pour it into a clean bowl, whisking well. Add the vanilla extract, if using, then place the bowl in iced water to cool completely.

Place the egg whites in a bowl with a small pinch of salt and whisk with an electric whisk until fluffy, just before the soft peak stage. Add the sugar, whisking continuously, until the white starts to become glossy, then add the lemon zest and stop.

Butter six 6cm pudding basins and coat the insides with sugar, turning them to coat them all over and shaking out the excess. Fill them to the brim with the egg mixture then place in the oven for 5 minutes. They should just be starting to rise when you take them out of the oven.

Leave to rest for 2 minutes then unmould each one on to the centre of a soup plate. Leave to cool completely.

Arrange the raspberries around the soft meringue, then pour over the crème anglaise and serve.

BRUNO'S TIPS

If the crème anglaise starts to curdle, immediately pour it into a blender, or use a hand blender and a tall container. Add two ice cubes and blitz until it becomes smooth again.

• • •

Strawberries or blueberries can replace the raspberries.

• • •

When whisking egg whites, leave the whites at room temperature for at least two hours beforehand as they will have more volume when whisked.

TARTE AUX POMMES

Do people realise how fortunate we are in the UK to have so many amazing varieties of apples? This is a question I often ask myself, especially when I see how little use is made of them on restaurant menus. But what is worse is the large quantity of foreign offerings found in shops. It seems that the supermarket lobby decided that good looks and limited variety was the way to achieve maximum profit and as a consequence many British varieties went out of favour; we are now in danger of losing them all together. I really would urge you to try different British varieties by seeking them out at farmers' markets and to support the great British apple. Or support local produce by checking the provenance when shopping in supermarkets, and buy British.

French people are usually very proud of their apple tart recipes and often families work on a recipe passed down through generations. Mine is a very simple one my mum used to make. I simply add a bit of rosemary and that's my generation's contribution. The recipe is now ready to be passed on.

Serves 6–8

500g puff pastry
15 Cox's Orange Pippin apples
    (see Bruno's Tips), peeled, cored,
    halved and cut into 2mm slices
20g butter
1 tbsp rosemary leaves
3 tbsp caster sugar
5 tbsp apricot jam
vanilla ice cream or crème fraîche,
    to serve

Almond cream
60g soft butter
75g icing sugar
1 tsp vanilla extract
2 drops of almond essence
1 egg
100g ground almonds
1 tsp cornflour
3 tbsp dark rum

Preheat the oven to 200°C/fan 180°C/Gas 6.

Start by making the almond cream. In a small bowl, whisk the butter with the sugar, vanilla and almond essence until the butter turns pale, then add the remaining ingredients for the cream. Whisk well and set aside.

Roll out the puff pastry on a lightly floured work surface to a 32cm round, then place on a baking sheet lined with non-stick baking paper.

Using the back of a small knife, draw a line 1cm in from the edge of the pastry all the way round. This will give the tart a border.

Prick inside the marked circle all over with a fork, then cover with the almond cream.

Starting from the outside, arrange the apples slices over the almond cream, overlapping them tightly so that only about 3mm of the previous slice is visible. Make a complete circle then start another circle, overlapping the previous one. Repeat this operation until the tart is complete. You should have 3–4 rings of apple.

In a small frying pan, melt the butter with the rosemary until foaming, then add the sugar. Stir, then remove from the heat and brush the mixture over the apples.

Bake for about 30 minutes or until the pastry is golden brown and the apples are well coloured around the edges. With a spatula, lift the tart carefully and check the bottom is cooked and crisp.

Heat the jam in a small saucepan. Sieve it if you want a very smooth glaze but for a more rustic finish there's no need, then brush over the tart.

Serve with vanilla ice cream or crème fraîche or simply as it is!

BRUNO'S TIPS

The best apple varieties for this tart are Cox's, Reinette and Egmont Russet.

• • •

Keep all the puff pastry trimmings. Do not mash them into a ball but place them on top of each other to preserve the layers in the pastry. Roll them out to about 3–4mm thick and as you are nearing this thickness add lots of brown sugar and cinnamon. Cut into fingers and bake at 200°C/fan 180°C/Gas 6 for about 8 minutes, until crisp. They make a great biscuit for afternoon tea!

• • •

If you are allergic to dairy or simply like your dessert a little lighter then spread a layer of Granny Smith compote under the sliced apples instead of the almond cream.

CHILLI & GINGER ROASTED PINEAPPLE

Throughout my eight years in Queensland, Australia, I enjoyed a lot of fruit – citrus fruits, mangoes and pineapple in particular. I spent two years cooking in the famous Berardo's restaurant in Noosa on the Sunshine Coast. The owners, Jim Berardo and Greg O'Brien, are so dedicated to the region that every year they put on one of the most amazing events: the Noosa Food and Wine Festival, which promotes good food from around Australia but particularly Queensland. The menu at their restaurant also reflects that dedication with the diversity of local bounties. This dessert is a homage to their passion!

Serves 6

1 ripe pineapple
50g butter
80g clear honey
1 red chilli, deseeded and very
    finely sliced
1 tsp finely chopped fresh root ginger
1 vanilla pod, split in half
juice of 2 limes

Frozen yoghurt
500g Greek yoghurt
juice of ½ lemon
4 tbsp good-quality dark rum
4 egg yolks
125g caster sugar
30ml hot water

I would recommend that you start making the frozen yoghurt the day before you want to serve it as that means you'll have less hassle on the day and there won't be any worry about whether it's completely frozen. Place the yoghurt, lemon juice and rum in a mixing bowl and mix well.

Place the egg yolks, sugar and hot water in another mixing bowl. Mix well with an electric whisk for 1 minute then place the bowl over a pan of gently simmering water, making sure the water does not touch the base of the bowl. Continue to whisk over the heat until the mixture becomes thick. At this stage, remove from the heat and keep whisking until it cools completely.

With a large plastic spatula or spoon, gently fold the egg mixture into the yoghurt. Do not overwork. Pour into six 5–6cm ramekins or a container of your choice and place in the freezer for a few hours to freeze completely.

Just before serving, peel the pineapple, cutting off all the brown spots, then cut in half lengthways. Cut each half lengthways again into three equal pieces. Cut off the hard core and pat dry.

In a large frying pan, heat the butter until foaming, then add the pineapple pieces. Cook until a nice golden colour all over, then add the honey, chilli, ginger, vanilla pod and lime juice. Give the pan a good swirl to coat the pineapple pieces all over for a couple of minutes or until the sauce in the pan thickens.

To serve, unmould the frozen yoghurts on to plates, place a piece of pineapple on each one and spoon the sauce all over.

CHOCOLATE & ORANGE SOUFFLE

Soufflé is one of those legendary posh French dishes that seem incredibly difficult to achieve. This recipe is one of the simplest I know and gives a brilliant result. If your ingredients are at room temperature when you start, and the moulds are buttered properly, then there is not much space for mistakes; you will impress your guests.

Serves 4

butter, to grease
90g caster sugar, plus extra to coat
*   the ramekins*
8 egg yolks
50g unsweetened cocoa powder,
*   plus extra to dust*
2 tablespoons whisky
½ tsp finely grated orange zest
10 egg whites
a pinch of salt

Preheat the oven to 200°C/fan 180°C/ Gas 6. With your finger, evenly butter the inside of four individual soufflé dishes, each 10cm in diameter and 5cm high. Put some sugar in one of the dishes and move it around to coat the whole surface. Tip all the excess sugar into another dish and coat it in the same way, then repeat with the other dishes. Set aside.

In a bowl, whisk together the egg yolks and 50g of the sugar until very smooth and white. Add the cocoa powder, whisky and orange zest and mix well.

In a large, clean bowl, whisk the egg whites with a tiny pinch of salt to soft peaks. Add the remaining 40g sugar and continue whisking until the mixture becomes firm but not too stiff.

Add a quarter of the egg whites to the egg yolk mixture. Mix with a whisk, then fold in the remaining egg whites (the best way is to use a pastry scraper).

Fill the prepared soufflé dishes with the mixture, right to the top, then above the rim by about 1cm. Be careful not to get any of the mixture on the edges of the dishes or the soufflés will stick to the dishes and will not rise evenly.

Place the dishes in a roasting tin and pour in about 1cm of hot water. Place the tin on top of the stove and bring the water to the boil, then transfer to the oven.

Bake for about 12 minutes, reducing the oven setting to 190°C/fan 170°C/ Gas 5 as soon as the soufflés start to rise.

When the soufflés are puffed up, remove them from their bain-marie of hot water, quickly dry the dishes and place on serving plates.

Dust some cocoa powder over the soufflés and serve immediately.

GOATS' MILK PANNA COTTA, WITH CANDIED TOMATOES

It's easy to forget that, botanically, a tomato is actually a fruit. At their best, well–ripened tomatoes are quite sweet, so there is nothing bizarre about using them in a dessert. Treated as in the recipe below they taste a bit like a damson; they look luxurious with a deep red colour and have an attractive shine. Like many people, as a child I used to have difficulties digesting cow's milk but goats' milk is a great substitute. It really works well in this dessert.

Serves 6

350ml goats' milk
1 tbsp milk powder
½ vanilla pod, split in half
grated zest of ¼ lemon
60g caster sugar
1½ gelatine leaves, soaked in cold
    water until soft
150ml whipping cream
2 tbsp natural yoghurt
vegetable oil, for greasing
limoncello, to serve
basil leaves, to serve (optional)

Candied tomatoes

6 ripe plum tomatoes or
    24 cherry tomatoes
50g icing sugar
6 tbsp light muscovado sugar
1 star anise, crushed
2 cardamom pods, crushed
scraped seeds of ½ vanilla pod
½ tsp finely grated orange zest

Start by making the candied tomatoes. Preheat the oven to 120°C/fan 100°C/ Gas ½. Have some iced water ready in a bowl. Make a small cross incision at the base of the tomatoes using a small sharp knife.

Plunge the tomatoes into boiling water for 8 seconds then place them in the iced water. When cool, peel the skin. Using a cocktail stick, spike each tomato all over 20 times. Place in a baking dish and dust with the icing sugar and add the other ingredients for the candied tomatoes. Roll the tomatoes to get them well covered with the ingredients then place in the oven for 3 hours. You will have to turn them from time to time and spoon over some of the liquid.

Bring the milk to the boil, whisk in the milk powder and add the vanilla pod, lemon zest and sugar. Remove from the heat and leave to infuse for 15 minutes. Add the soaked gelatine and place the bowl in iced water to cool.

Whip the cream until soft peaks form. When the milk is completely cold and just starting to set, whisk in the yoghurt, then fold in the whipped cream.

Lightly oil six dariole moulds, about 5–6cm in diameter, then pour the mixture into the moulds. Cover with cling film and place in the fridge for 2 hours to set.

Unmould the panna cottas by turning them upside down over the serving plate, keeping the mould about 3cm above the plate. Gently push the sides of the panna cotta with two fingers to get some air inside – this will release it.

To serve, place a panna cotta on one side of each plate and the tomatoes on the other. At the table pour a splash of limoncello over each plate and scatter over a few basil leaves, if using.

BRUNO'S TIPS

If tomatoes are not in season or ripe enough then you can use strawberries or even stewed rhubarb instead.

LIGHT CHRISTMAS PIE

Having Christmas pudding on the 25th December is an old tradition, dating back to medieval England. The blend of dried fruits, brown sugar, cinnamon, nutmeg and whisky creates a splendid array of flavours with depth. I love to mix Christmas pudding with an apple compote to create this lighter dessert that still captures the Christmas spirit.

Serves 8–10

6 Granny Smith apples, peeled, cored
*   and cut into chunks*
juice of 1 lemon
1 x 450g Christmas pudding, crumbled
demerara sugar, to finish
500g crème fraîche, to serve

Pastry
650g plain flour, plus extra for dusting
grated zest of 1 orange
250g butter, at room temperature,
*   plus extra, melted, for glazing*
*   the pastry*
2 eggs, plus 2 egg yolks
3 tbsp iced water

Start by making the pastry. Put the flour, orange zest and butter in the food processor and process until the mixture resembles coarse breadcrumbs. At this stage, add the eggs, yolks and water. Process again until the mixture just comes together, no more.

Place the dough on a lightly floured work surface and knead with the palm of your hands until smooth. Shape it into a ball and flatten it slightly, then wrap the dough in cling film and place in the fridge for 30 minutes.

Preheat the oven to 195°C/fan 175°C/Gas 5½. Place the apples in a pan with the lemon juice and 50ml of water. Cook gently over a low heat until the apples soften. At this stage, add the crumbled pudding. Stir well, then transfer the mixture to a flat dish or tray to cool down.

Cut off a third of the pastry, then place both pieces on a lightly floured surface. Roll out the pastry into two circles, about 1cm thick. Place the larger one into a 35cm x 23cm, deep pie dish, making sure it takes the shape of the dish. Fill with the apple mixture then cover with the other piece of pastry. Pinch the edges to seal the pie and cut a hole in the middle for the steam to escape. Brush the pastry with melted butter and sprinkle with demerara sugar. Bake in the oven for about 30 minutes until golden brown. Serve with crème fraîche.

SALTED CARAMEL & COCONUT MACAROONS

These puffed little almondy biscuits, displayed in carefully arranged lines of pastel shades in patisseries, seem to have stolen the hearts of a legion of fans around the world. They look so pretty and taste delicious. The hard, crunchy biscuit shell belies the chewy, nutty centre, but the delight doesn't end there as the two little biscuits are sandwiched together with a deliciously sweet filling.

Makes about 18 macaroons

200g icing sugar
125g ground almonds
40g desiccated coconut
3 egg whites, at room temperature
    (see Bruno's Tip)
a pinch of salt
40g caster sugar
½ tsp lemon juice

Filling
60g caster sugar
60ml double cream
2 pinches of Maldon sea salt
140g good-quality dark chocolate
1 tbsp dark rum

Place the icing sugar, almonds and half the coconut in a food processor. Process until very fine then pour into a bowl.

Place the egg whites in a clean bowl with a pinch of salt, then whisk with an electric whisk until soft peaks form. Add the sugar and whisk for another minute until stiff peaks form. The mixture should be really thick. Add the lemon, continuing to whisk for 10 seconds. Sprinkle half the almond mixture over and fold in with a plastic spatula until just combined, then add the other half in the same way – do not over work it. Transfer the mix to a piping bag fitted with a 15mm plain nozzle.

Line a flat baking sheet with greaseproof paper. Pipe the macaroon shells by placing the nozzle against the tray, then gently pushing the mixture out of the bag, controlling the flow, to create a small mound, 3cm in diameter. Leave a gap of at least 3cm between each shell and repeat the piping until all the mixture has been used up (you should get about 36 circles), then sprinkle the tops with the remaining coconut.

Preheat the oven to 145°C/fan 125°C/ Gas 1½. Leave the macaroons on the tray in a cool place for about 30 minutes for the characteristic 'crust' or 'skin' to form. Place the baking tray on to a second baking tray (see Bruno's Tips), then place in the oven for about 15 minutes, until the macaroons are crispy and they lift off the paper easily when lifted with a palette knife.

Remove from the oven and carefully transfer the shells (still on the greaseproof paper) to a wire rack to cool.

For the filling, heat the sugar in a small saucepan over a medium heat to a dark caramel then gently pour in the cream, being careful it doesn't splash, add the salt, and stir, then remove from the heat.

Add the chocolate and mix again, until the chocolate has melted. Pour into a small bowl to cool completely, then add the rum, mixing well. Place in the fridge for about 10 minutes for the filling to firm up a little.

Carefully lift a macaroon shell off the paper. Holding a shell in one hand, use a palette knife to delicately spread some of the filling over the flat side then sandwich it with another shell. Repeat to use up all the filling mixure.

These macaroons look fantastic served on a coloured plate, lightly dusted with icing sugar.

BRUNO'S TIPS

To create more volume in your egg whites, separate the yolks from the whites four days before making your macaroons (if possible!), then keep covered in the fridge. This will mean the mixture will have more air and the macaroons will have a lovely domed shape.

• • •

Baking sheets for home use are often quite thin, which means that when the macaroon shells are placed in the oven, the heat from the oven gets to the delicate mixture very fast. Doubling up the thickness of the baking surface helps to reduce the intensity of the heat and the macaroons will bake more slowly and evenly, developing their chewy interior rather than being crunchy all the way through.

KAFFIR LIME ICED PARFAIT WITH LIQUORICE FIGS

Kaffir limes have such a beautiful, interesting fragrance. Like yuzu from Japan or calamansi from the Philippines, these citrus fruits are now more easily obtainable and bring interesting new flavours to our menus. Nevertheless, Kaffir limes can still prove difficult to find and can also be very expensive. However, I've found a trick to save the day. I use Kaffir lime leaves, which are very widely available, together with normal lime juice and it works wonders, resulting in a pretty close match. The figs poached in liquorice bring an interesting aniseed and sweet flavour, which contrasts perfectly with the elegant 'perfume' of the citrus.

Serves 6

500ml double cream
125g caster sugar
120ml water
3 Kaffir lime leaves, very finely chopped
6 egg yolks
½ tsp finely grated lime zest
juice of 2 limes
6 mint tops, to decorate

Poached figs
400ml water
60g sweetened liquorice
1 bay leaf
juice of ¼ lemon
80g caster sugar
6 figs

You will also need a cooking thermometer

For the parfait, whip the cream until stiff peaks form, then set aside. Line six 140ml dariole moulds or ramekins with cling film.

Place the sugar, water and Kaffir lime leaves in a small saucepan over a medium heat and cook until the sugar dissolves and the mixture reaches 121°C on your thermometer ('soft-ball' stage).

Meanwhile, set a mixing bowl over a pan of barely simmering water, add the egg yolks and 6 tablespoons of hot water and immediately start whisking with an electric mixer until pale and fluffy. Continue whisking until the Kaffir lime and sugar mixture reaches the soft ball stage, then pour this mixture in a fine stream over the yolks, whisking continuously.

Remove the bowl from the heat and continue to whisk until cool. When completely cool, whisk in the lime zest and juice. Gently fold the whipped cream into the parfait until just combined, then pour into the moulds. Place in the freezer to set completely. This should take about 4 hours depending on your freezer.

Poach the figs. Place the water, liquorice, bay leaf, lemon juice and sugar in a pan and bring to the boil. Boil for 5 minutes, then add the figs and lower the heat to a simmer. The figs should take about 6–8 minutes to poach – they should be very tender when pierced with the tip of a sharp knife. Remove from the heat and leave the figs to cool in their poaching liquid.

To serve, unmould the iced parfaits on to cold plates, add a poached fig and decorate with a mint sprig.

BRUNO'S TIPS

This dessert is lovely served with a bit of raspberry or strawberry coulis.

STRAWBERRIES ON ELDERFLOWER JELLY, & CHAMPAGNE

I find it interesting how we associate smells with different things in our life. When I smell lavender, I think of Provence – of fields in full sunlight with the Mistral sweeping its way to the coast. When I smell elderflower, I think of the English countryside; its lush palette of greens along country lanes and pretty pubs in the valley. The scent of elderflowers and strawberries is pure English summer. Once, I asked one of my chefs to smell strawberries and tell me what it made him think of. He closed his eyes, inhaled the smell of the fruits deeply, then opened his eyes slowly and said: 'Wimbledon, chef!'

Serves 4

900g strawberries, hulled
3 tbsp elderflower cordial
3 tbsp water
1 tsp lemon juice
1½ gelatine leaves, soaked in water
    until soft then squeezed of
    excess water
4 balls of strawberry or raspberry sorbet,
    to serve
8 basil leaves, to decorate
Champagne, a splash per serving, or
    more (!), to serve

Slice 500g of the strawberries very finely, place in a small pan with the cordial, water and lemon juice. Mix well then leave to stand for 20 minutes, mixing from time to time. Cover the pan tightly with cling film then place over a low heat.

Gently swirl the pan from time to time to mix it well. After about 10 minutes, remove from the heat and leave to stand for another 5 minutes.

Pass the liquid through a sieve lined with muslin or a tea strainer set over a bowl. Stir in the soaked gelatine, then place the bowl inside another bowl of iced water to cool.

Place the remaining whole strawberries in four serving glasses.

Pour the cold juice over and place in the fridge for an hour to set.

To serve, spoon the sorbet over each jelly, decorate with the basil leaves, then pour the Champagne over the leaves and sorbet. Serve immediately.

BRUNO'S TIPS

Now that England produces sparkling wine of excellent quality, try it with this dish, it will be a lovely discovery!

STRAWBERRY & BALSAMIC JAM

I am often asked where I find my inspiration; how do I come up with a dish? Some people have this romantic notion of a chef staying late after work (having already worked a 14-hour day) in their kitchen to develop new concoctions like a mad scientist. Well, I am sorry to disappoint but it's a bit less original than that, for me at least. Usually it starts with the seasons – what's available at the time of the year – and what we can afford. I then look at what I have done in the past. Do I want something new or should I revisit a popular dish? Then the creative process starts in my mind, coming and going during the day or sometimes over a few days, until my mind is clear and happy! The dish will then have a chance to find its way on to the menu but only if it can be balanced with the other dishes.

I created this dish after a trip to Italy where I was served strawberry ice cream with a dash of old balsamic vinegar. Two days later the jam was in the jars!

Makes 1.2kg

2kg ripe strawberries, hulled and
*   halved, or cut into quarters if large*
1.2kg jam sugar
150ml orange juice
2 tbsp lemon juice
⅓ tsp freshly ground black pepper
200ml balsamic vinegar

Place the strawberries in a bowl and add the sugar, the orange and lemon juice and pepper. Mix well and cover with cling film. Place in the fridge to marinate for 2 hours.

Place the strawberries and their marinade juices in a pan and bring to the boil, then lower the heat to a simmer. Skim the surface and discard all the foam that rises, and simmer for 30 minutes.

Meanwhile, place the balsamic vinegar in a clean saucepan and bring to the boil. Boil until the vinegar is reduced by about three-quarters, with 50ml remaining. Remove from the heat.

Drain the strawberries in a colander set over a bowl or pan, then reduce the syrup to two–thirds of the strawberry volume. Return the cooked strawberries to the pan along with the reduced balsamic vinegar, bring to the boil, then remove from the heat.

The jam should have quite a thick consistency but should not be completely set. Transfer the jam to sterilised jars and store the unopened jars in a cool place for up to 2 months. Keep in the fridge once opened.

BRUNO'S TIPS

When buying your sugar, look for jam sugar that contains fruit pectin as this will help your jam to set.

FRESH RASPBERRY MOUSSE WITH BASIL SYRUP

For this recipe, I've given you two versions: a classic one that is rich and more textured, and one that is very light, simple and clean. You will have to try both to decide which you prefer, but please note that the simpler one requires an ISI cream whipper or soda siphon and the gas cartridges that go with it.

The basil syrup is a lovely, unusual touch with a 'trick' in the recipe to guarantee a stronger basil flavour; it's a simple colourful twist!

Serves 6

Simple option
500ml raspberry coulis
2 gelatine leaves, soaked in cold water
*   until soft*
juice of ½ lemon
300ml double cream
3 tbsp raspberry liqueur
*   (such as Chambord)*

Classic option
300ml raspberry coulis
1 gelatine leaf, soaked in cold water
*   until soft*
½ tsp lemon juice
80g caster sugar
2 egg whites
150ml double cream
2 tbsp raspberry liqueur
*   (such as Chambord)*
200g fresh raspberries, crushed

Basil syrup
100g jam sugar
100ml water
1 bunch of basil, roughly chopped
2 tbsp Pernod (the 'trick' ingredient)

You will also need a cooking thermometer

Start by making the basil syrup. Bring the sugar and water to a boil in a small saucepan, then add the basil. Remove from the heat and blitz in a blender with two ice cubes until smooth. Pour into a bowl placed in iced water, then stir in the Pernod. Chill until ready to use.

For the simple mousse option, heat 100ml of the raspberry coulis in a small saucepan until warm, then stir in the soaked gelatine. Pour into a bowl and add the remaining ingredients, including the remaining coulis. Mix well then pour the mixture into the ISI bottle, close it well with two gas cartridges and place in the fridge for about 15 minutes. It is then ready to use.

For the classic option, heat 100ml of the raspberry coulis in a small saucepan until warm, then stir in the soaked gelatine. Pour into a bowl and add the remaining coulis and lemon juice, then place in the fridge.

In a small pan, boil the sugar with 50ml of water until it reaches 121°C ('soft-ball' stage).

Meanwhile, whisk the egg whites with a mixer or an electric hand whisk until the whisk leaves a ribbon trail when lifted out, then pour in the sugar syrup in a fine stream, whisking continuously until the mixture cools completely.

Whip the cream until the whisk leaves a ribbon trail when lifted out, then add the liqueur.

Transfer the coulis to a large mixing bowl, whisk well then fold in the whipped cream and finally the egg whites. Fold in the crushed raspberries.

To serve, pour or squirt some mousse into the bottom of six tall glasses, then cover with about a tablespoon of the basil syrup then another layer of mousse, and so on until you fill the glasses.

HERB OIL
USER-FRIENDLY
PRESERVED LEMONS
AILLADE TOULOUSAINE
RED WINE &
GREEN PEPPERCORN MUSTARD
GREEN TOMATO CHUTNEY
DUKKAH
ROUILLE SAUCE
ROQUEFORT & YOGHURT
SPREAD
MUSTARD APRICOTS
MOROCCAN
SWEET & SOUR DRESSING
VIETNAMESE DRESSING

FAMILY HOUSE
VINAIGRETTE
WALNUT VINAIGRETTE
SAUCE GRIBICHE
BECHAMEL SAUCE
FRESH PASTA DOUGH

BASICS

HERB OIL

This is a garden in a bottle. The deep-green colour of this oil looks amazing on any dish. When the herbs are very lightly cooked in boiling water they still hold their flavour but all the chlorophyll is preserved, giving the oil its attractive colour. The recipe below makes a fairly small quantity but the process is so simple that it is better to make it more often so that it's fresher.

Makes 150ml

½ tsp salt
150ml olive oil
3 tbsp chopped tarragon
5 tbsp flat-leaf parsley
3 tbsp chopped chives

Place the olive oil in the fridge and the jug of your blender in the freezer for 30 minutes.

Bring a small pan of water to the boil and add the salt. Plunge the tarragon into the boiling water, followed by the parsley 5 seconds later, then the chives another 5 seconds later. Leave for 10 seconds then drain in a colander and squeeze out any excess water. Transfer the herbs to the cold blender with the oil then blitz to a smooth texture. Stop as soon as it's smooth so the heat from the friction in the blender doesn't heat the herbs, otherwise they will lose their colour. At this stage you can either pass the oil through a muslin cloth to strain the herbs, or not, if you prefer. If you don't, then simply leave the oil to rest in a tall glass for the remaining herb fibres to settle at the bottom, making it easy to separate. I personally leave it.

BRUNO'S TIPS

If you're using shop-bought herbs, it is a great idea to buy the herbs that are sold in pots. The yield is much better and they are as fresh as can be.

USER-FRIENDLY PRESERVED LEMONS

Like many French people, I love North African food. I remember staying with friends in Casablanca and being served a chicken, preserved lemon and olive tagine made by a local lady. My first bite into the chicken revealed a beautiful succession of flavours. I then had a second bite and in my excitement bit into a piece of lemon that I embarrassingly spat out into my hands. I loved the flavour the lemon was giving but could not eat a piece, so that got me thinking… The result is something I have called 'user-friendly preserved lemons' because, made this way, it can be spread over a roast or grilled chicken two-thirds into the cooking time; it can be added to tagines; or used as a marinade for lamb kebabs and there won't be any lemony surprises. I always have a jar in my fridge.

Makes 2 x 300ml jars

5 lemons, unwaxed if possible, finely
    sliced and pips removed
4 tbsp sea salt
5 garlic cloves
½ cinnamon stick
1 star anise
1 red chilli
1 bay leaf
½ tsp cumin seeds, toasted
150ml olive oil, plus extra to layer
2 tbsp caster sugar

Lay the lemon slices on a tray or trays lined with cling film and sprinkle with the salt. Place in the freezer and leave for 24 hours.

The next day, allow the lemons to defrost for about 10 minutes. Put the lemon, any juices from the defrosting, and all remaining ingredients in a pan set over a medium heat. Bring to a simmer, mix well and cover with a lid. Lower the heat to a very gentle simmer, then leave to stew for about 45 minutes. Remove from the heat and leave to rest for 30 minutes.

There are now two ways to proceed depending on your taste:

Remove the cinnamon stick and purée the mixture in a food processor then transfer to a sterilised jar.

Whisk it firmly to break all the pieces down, then fill a sterilised jar.

When the jar is full, pour a small layer of olive oil over the top. Leave to cool completely, then store in the fridge for up to 2 months.

AILLADE TOULOUSAINE

For a long time garlic has been recognised for its diverse medicinal properties. The Egyptians, Greeks and Romans already knew of its antibiotic qualities and these days, garlic extract is used in medicines. When I was a teenager, my brother and I came up with a troublesome idea. When our large crop of garlic was ready, it was harvested and hung by the stalks under the roof of our garden shed. When dried, the stalks were like layers of paper, so we decided they should be 'smokeable'. That was the start of many headaches and sore throats, which my mother could not understand and tried to cure by having us eat raw garlic cloves three times a day! So eat more garlic and you should be more healthy…

Serves 6

100g walnuts
6 large garlic cloves
½ sage leaf
1 tsp wholegrain mustard
2 tbsp water
100ml walnut oil
3 tbsp vegetable oil
1 tbsp chopped flat-leaf parsley
1 tbsp chopped chives
salt and black pepper

Using a pestle and mortar, pound together the walnuts, garlic and sage to a fine purée. (If you don't have a pestle and mortar, use a blender.)

Add the mustard and water then add the oils in a fine stream, pounding and moving the mixture around the mortar to combine thoroughly. The mixture will become thick like a runny mayonnaise. At this stage, add the parsley and chives and seasoning to taste and it's ready!

BRUNO'S TIPS

If you're not keen on the powerful taste of raw garlic then you can split each clove in two and boil them in water for 2 minutes, it will tame the taste.

• • •

This sauce is excellent with a lamb roast and often we used to have it with a big platter of crudités and some lovely crusty bread.

RED WINE & GREEN PEPPERCORN MUSTARD

Utterly superb with a steak or a roasted piece of pork, this flavoured mustard is very versatile and useful to have to hand in the fridge.

Makes 280ml

200ml red wine
3 tbsp port
100g Dijon mustard
100g wholegrain mustard
1 tbsp green peppercorns, crushed
1 tbsp chopped tarragon

Place the red wine and port in a small saucepan. Bring to the boil and reduce until only a quarter is left, then remove from the heat and set aside to cool.

Once cool, add the two mustards, crushed peppercorns and tarragon, mix well then spoon into a sterilised jar. Store in the fridge for up to 1 month.

GREEN TOMATO CHUTNEY

Years ago, before I left for Australia, I used to have an allotment in London. The neighbours in my street were very nice and we became good friends, often meeting in the communal gardens for a glass of wine – sometimes a bottle – or around a table with a nice meal. Our garden harvest became quite competitive and we decided to organise a summer tomato chutney competition. This was the winning recipe.

Makes 3–4 x 300ml jars

3 tbsp olive oil
3 garlic cloves, chopped
1 tbsp grated fresh root ginger
2 green chillies, chopped
½ tbsp coriander seeds, toasted and
    pounded to a fine powder
200g onions, peeled and finely chopped
1.5kg green tomatoes, finely chopped
300g marrow, diced
150g golden raisins
300g demerara sugar
400ml tarragon vinegar
¼ tsp ground turmeric

Secret ingredients
1 tbsp lime pickle, very finely chopped
1 x 255g bottle HP sauce
2 tbsp Worcestershire sauce

In a large pan, heat the olive oil over a medium heat, then add the garlic, ginger, chilli, coriander and onions. Mix well with a wooden spoon and cook for about 5 minutes, until the onions soften a bit, then add all the remaining ingredients. Bring to the boil, skim the surface and lower the heat to a simmer.

Leave to simmer for about 2 hours, stirring occasionally until the chutney has thickened. Remove from the heat, then pour into sterilised jars and seal. The chutney can be kept unopened for up to 6 months. Once opened, store in the fridge for up to 1 month.

BRUNO'S TIPS

You can accelerate the cooking process if it's more convenient to cook it quickly rather than wait 2 hours. After 1 hour, pour the ingredients into a colander set over a bowl. Pour the liquid back into the pan and reduce to a syrup, then replace the strained ingredients. Bring it back to the boil, then remove from the heat and transfer to the sterilised jars.

DUKKAH

Originally from Egypt, this dish, which is full of character, is a must-have in your pantry. I first discovered the interesting mix of nuts, seeds and spices in Australia where it's popularly used as an accompaniment to an aperitif, served with soft bread and good olive oil as a dip (you dip the bread in the oil, then the dukkah). However, it's incredibly versatile and can be sprinkled over vegetables, purées, salads, cheese, toast, grilled meats, or just about anything to make a dish come alive.

Makes about 225g

80g nibbed almonds
80g peeled hazelnuts
40g sesame seeds
½ tsp coriander seeds
½ tsp cumin seeds
2 pinches of dried chilli
1 tsp Maldon sea salt
2 pinches of allspice
½ tsp celery salt
⅓ tsp black pepper
½ dried oregano

Toast the almonds and hazelnuts until dark golden, then leave to cool completely.

In a clean frying pan, heat the sesame, coriander and cumin seeds until the fragrant smell of the oils comes through, then pour into a pestle and mortar and add the chilli, salt, allspice, celery salt, black pepper and oregano. Crush with the mortar until very fine.

Chop the almonds and hazelnuts in the food processor but not too fine.

Now mix the ground spices and nuts together. Your dukkah is ready to be enjoyed with extra-virgin oil and bread.

Store the dukkah in an airtight container in a cool place.

ROUILLE SAUCE

Traditionally served with bouillabaisse (see page 127), this sauce is also delicious served with any grilled fish or simply as a dip with toasted baguette.

Makes about 350ml

100g Desiree potatoes, peeled and cut
    into large chunks
a pinch of saffron
1 tbsp lemon juice
2 egg yolks
1 tsp Dijon mustard
150ml olive oil
1 tsp harissa paste
⅓ red chilli, deseeded and very
    finely chopped
4 garlic cloves, very finely chopped
salt and black pepper

Place the potatoes in a large pan, cover with cold water, bring to the boil and simmer for 12–15 minutes or until tender. Drain and mash well with a potato masher.

Soak the saffron in the lemon juice and 2 teaspoons of water.

Place the egg yolks in a medium bowl with the mustard, whisk well then slowly pour in the olive oil in a thin stream, whisking continuously. Add the mashed potato, the saffron and its soaking liquid, the harissa, chilli, garlic and seasoning and whisk well.

BRUNO'S TIPS

Traditionally, a rouille sauce is made with bread but I like to replace this with potatoes, which give the sauce a velvety texture.

ROQUEFORT & YOGHURT SPREAD

For me, this spread is the ultimate afternoon tea-break snack. It's delicious spread on crusty bread or multigrain crispbread. Fresh breakfast radishes and walnut can be added as a topping and it becomes a simple, flavoursome start to a meal.

Serves 4 as a spread

300g Greek yoghurt
100g Roquefort cheese

Place the yoghurt to drain in a colander lined with a muslin cloth set over a bowl. If you put a weight over it, such as a plate topped with a tin, it will help to speed up the process.

When the yoghurt loses a third of its volume (after about 20 minutes), spoon it out of the muslin into a bowl. Add the Roquefort cheese and use a fork to mash it down and mix to a thin spread, or you could do this in an electric mixer.

BRUNO'S TIPS

This is also delicious stirred through pasta.

MUSTARD APRICOTS

Italian mustard fruits (*mostarda di frutta*) are now well known. They are quite particular but great in their classic pairing with pumpkin dishes and with cold meats. I personally find them remarkable with blue cheeses. There is one problem and that's their price: they are quite expensive, especially if you don't use them often, so the best alternative is to make your own. And I prefer my version to shop-bought versions as their texture is softer and they do not taste so sweet.

I once served my version to one of my Italian friends who only buys imported products and swears by them. He said mine were the best *mostarda di frutta* he'd ever tasted and that I must give him the address of the place where I'd bought them. I enjoyed the pleasure and happiness he was expressing so much that I could not divulge the truth and told him the production was so small that I had to keep it a secret. But the truth is now out – sorry Angelo!

Makes 800g

300ml white wine vinegar
200g caster sugar
½ cinnamon stick
2 tbsp English mustard powder
2 drops of almond essence
500g dried apricots

Bring the vinegar, sugar and cinnamon to the boil in a pan and boil for 30 seconds, then whisk in the mustard powder and almond essence.

Add the dried apricots, lower the heat to a gentle simmer, cover with a lid and cook for 1 hour – the liquid will reduce and become syrupy.

Remove from the heat, then pour into hot sterilised jars. Store in the fridge for up to 1 month.

MOROCCAN SWEET & SOUR DRESSING

This dressing is particularly good served with a warm salad in winter but it can be used as a baste for roast chicken: simply baste the bird with the dressing 10 minutes before the end of the cooking time.

Makes about 400ml

1 tsp coriander seeds
1 tsp cumin seeds
200ml olive oil
50ml lemon juice
50ml orange juice
2 tbsp clear honey
2 garlic cloves, chopped
1 tsp User-friendly Preserved Lemons
  (see page 226)
½ tsp harissa
salt and black pepper

In a dry frying pan, heat the coriander seeds for 30 seconds over a medium heat, then add the cumin seeds for 1 minute. Immediately remove from the heat and grind in a pestle and mortar to a fine powder.

Place all the ingredients in a bowl and whisk well then pour into a bottle or a glass jar. Close and shake well before using. Store in the fridge.

VIETNAMESE DRESSING

I use this recipe for the Sweet Soy Braised Beef Cheeks (see pages 119–20), but it's a tasty dressing to go on any Asian-style salad, especially served with rice vermicelli.

Makes 125ml

4 tbsp sesame oil
4 tbsp olive oil
4 tbsp lime juice
2 tbsp sweet chilli sauce
1 tbsp fish sauce
2 garlic cloves, sliced
2 Kaffir lime leaves, very finely chopped
½ tbsp finely grated fresh root ginger

Place all the ingredients in a blender and blitz for 20 seconds. Shake well before using.

BRUNO'S TIPS

The fish sauce can be omitted if you don't like it but you will need to season the dressing with salt or some salted anchovies instead.

FAMILY HOUSE VINAIGRETTE

Everyone seems to have a favourite dressing; we always have a bottle ready to be shaken in our family kitchen. I am often asked how I make my dressing and usually say a few ingredients and a little secret. When the secret is out, people are definitely surprised... But it's so good.

Makes 250ml

100ml olive oil
3 tbsp vegetable oil
4 tbsp good-quality red wine vinegar
2 garlic cloves, crushed
1 tsp Dijon mustard
2 tbsp water
1 tsp Maggi liquid seasoning
salt and black pepper

Place all the ingredients in a small bottle or jar. Close tightly and shake well.

Shake well again before use. Store in the fridge.

WALNUT VINAIGRETTE

My mother only used walnut oil from the Périgord region on special occasions as it was expensive, but we always had walnuts in their shells on hand at home because we used to go foraging for them and they were plentiful in the area. Sometimes my mother used to crush them in a pestle and mortar with grapeseed oil to make her own oil – much more resourceful and cost-effective!

Makes 475ml

100ml walnut oil
200ml grapeseed oil
125ml good-quality red wine vinegar
50ml water
1 tbsp Dijon mustard
½ tsp caster sugar
salt and black pepper

Whisk all the ingredients together then pour into a 500ml bottle or large jar. Close and shake well before using. Store in the fridge.

SAUCE GRIBICHE

Sauce gribiche is a classic egg-based French sauce usually served with cold meats or poached fish. It is very much like tartare sauce with a slight difference: tartare sauce is basically a mayonnaise with raw egg yolks folded in with the other ingredients; in a gribiche the egg yolks are used cooked and less oil is added.

Serves 6

4 eggs
1 tbsp Dijon mustard
½ tbsp white wine vinegar
6 tbsp grapeseed oil
1 tbsp capers, roughly chopped
1 tbsp finely chopped gherkins
1 tbsp roughly chopped parsley
1 tbsp roughly chopped chervil
1 tsp finely chopped chives
salt and black pepper

Boil the eggs in salted water for 8 minutes, then cool completely in iced water.

Peel the eggs, then separate the yolks from the whites. Chop the whites and set aside.

Place the yolks in a small bowl and crush to a fine paste with the mustard, then add the vinegar and mix well. Pour the oil into the egg yolks in a fine stream, whisking continuously, then fold in the remaining ingredients. Season with salt and pepper, to taste.

BRUNO'S TIPS

I like to fold in a spoonful of crème fraîche to my gribiche. It's not at all classic but is delicious.

BECHAMEL SAUCE

This is one of the simplest sauces to make and also one of the most versatile because lots of flavours can be added to it, such as pesto, mushrooms and mustard. Pour the sauce over pasta, roast vegetables or leftover roast chicken and finish with grated Gruyère or Cheddar cheese – it will make an excellent gratin or bake.

Makes about 500ml

40g butter
40g plain flour
500ml milk
salt
3 pinches of freshly grated nutmeg

In a saucepan, melt the butter until foaming, then add the flour. Whisk well and cook for 30 seconds on a low heat then set aside.

In a separate pan bring the milk to the boil, then pour over the butter and flour mix (roux), whisking continuously over a medium heat. When the sauce starts to bubble, lower the heat to a gentle simmer and leave to cook for 5 minutes. Season with salt and nutmeg.

FRESH PASTA DOUGH

Pasta-making is relatively easy and fun, and what's more, eating your labour of love is very rewarding. It is said that Italians eat an average of 25kg of pasta per person each year.

At the bistrot I only use fresh pasta for making stuffed pasta such as ravioli and tortellini, but a nice fresh pasta with a meat ragout is great.

Makes about 500g

500g '00' flour, plus extra to dust
2 eggs
6 egg yolks
1 tbsp olive oil

Place the flour on a work surface and form a well in the centre. Place the eggs and yolks in a bowl with the oil. Whisk well with a fork then pour into the middle of the well.

Slowly, using the tips of your fingers, bring the flour into the centre and mix until the dough comes together.

Lightly flour the work surface and knead the dough with the palms of your hands until it becomes smooth and silky. Make a ball with the dough, then flatten a little. Wrap in cling film and place in the fridge to rest for at least 1 hour. The dough is then ready to use.

BRUNO'S TIPS

If you don't have a pasta machine, you can use a rolling pin to roll out your dough – you will just need a lot of patience!

ACKNOWLEDGEMENTS

Thank you.

A lot of the recipes have been kindly (and bravely) tasted by friends.
I would like to say thank you to all of them and hope they enjoy the book.

In England:
Laura McPate
Reica Gray
Marc Andre Richard and Trevor Haynes
Harriet Close

In Australia:
Ramma Prasad
Amada Reboul
Sue Truscott
Greg Adermann
The Russell family

In the US:
Liz Erlinger

In Canada:
Lark Masney

I would also like to thank all the other people that have helped me in the
making of this book: Sarah Lavelle, my editor at Ebury for her patience;
Jonathan Lovekin, whose talent as a photographer I greatly admire; Will Webb
for his fantastic design; my daughters Laeticia, Laura and Chloe for inspiring
some of these recipes; my wife Catherine for helping to coordinate this project,
for her decryption of my scribblings and her support; and all the friends who
have shared eating those recipes on many very long Sunday lunches!

INDEX

A

aillade toulousaine 227

almond cream 202–5

anchovy, pissaladière with marinated sardine
   fillets 52–4

apple

   light Christmas pie 210–11

   tarte aux pommes 202–5

apricot

   mustard 233

   vegetable couscous 149

Armagnac & prune sticky pudding 186–7

artichoke

   baked globe, with goats' cheese 22–3

   Jerusalem

      plum & wild rabbit tagine 140–1

      vegetable couscous 149

asparagus

   cocotte of spring & summer vegetables
      160–1

   new potatoes & green gazpacho with
      salmon confit 115

   roasted with meat jus 60–1

aubergine

   grilled & smoked, with creamed citrus
      dressing, pomegranate & fresh mint
      30–1

   lime pickle & yoghurt, with toasted
      almonds 156–7

   Provencal tian 162–3

   stuffed 76–7

   vegetable couscous 149

B

bacon

   & bread pudding 90–2

   & chicken liver stuffing 121–3

   chicken terrine Nicoise-style 49–50

   Gorgonzola & walnut stuffed mushrooms
      37

   mint, celery & broad beans 174

balsamic jam, & strawberry 217

balsamic syrup, pea pancakes & poached
   egg 38–9

basil

   purée (pistou) 108–10

   syrup, with fresh raspberry mousse
      218–19

béchamel sauce 238

beef

   my father's côte de boeuf 132–5

   my spaghetti Bordelaise 139

   sweet soy braised cheeks, with mango
      salad 118–20

beetroot

   baked in hay 172–3

   ravioli 1997 62–6

berries, red, & red cabbage, braised 168

black pudding & Scotch egg salad with
   horseradish dressing 78–9

blackberry sauce, raw & cooked cauliflower
   & wild pigeon 136–8

blue cheese & turkey triple decker croque
   monsieur 145

bouillabaisse, sustainable 127–31

bread

   & bacon pudding 90–2

   wholemeal, & lemon & spinach
      dumplings in tomato broth 69

Brie, baked, with potatoes & ham, flambéed
   with gin 102–3

broad bean

   with celery, bacon & mint 174

   cocotte of spring & summer vegetables
      160–1

   quinoa & Treviso salad 124–5

   vegetable couscous 149

Brussels sprouts, ginger & soy, with roast
   partridge 96–7

butter

   burnt, & peach tart 196–8

   garlic & parsley 121–3

   herb 20–1

C

cabbage

   pickled 100–1, 175

   red, & red berries, braised 168

   shredded Chinese, cashew nut & duck
      salad 85–7

calves' liver, grilled marinated, with green
   tomato chutney & polenta 148

caramel, salted, & coconut macaroons
   212–14

dumplings, wholemeal bread, lemon & spinach 69

WHITE ONION SOUP ASPARAGUS
RAW FENNEL & COURGETTE PRUNE & ARMAGNAC
PEA SOUP A LA FRANCAISE QUAIL
CHAKCHOUKA PRUNE
WITH MERGUEZ CHICKEN LEMON POLENTA TERRINE SNAILS
POTTED OXTAIL SMOKED CHICKEN
CRAB, CORN, GINGER GRAND MARNIER
CHILLI RISOTTO ROLLED LAMB
GOATS' CHEESE BEETROOT RAVIOLI
SLOW-BAKED ONIONS PEARS, ROQUEFORT
PEA PANCAKES CREPES SUZETTE
SAUCE GRIBICHE GREEN LENTILS JAM
LOBSTER SALAD «WATEGO»
SMOOTH CHICKEN RIZ
LIVER PATE SALAD WITH HORSERADISH SALAD
DRESSING PICKLED CABBAGE
PARTRIDGE
GORGONZOLA, WALNUT &
BACON STUFFED MUSHROOMS POACHED PEARS
PISSALADIERE WITH VIETNAMESE DRESSING
MARINATED SARDINE FILLETS PROVENCAL TIAN
KAFFIR LIME ICED PARFAIT SALTED CARAMEL
SOUSED MACKEREL EGG PATE DUE